THE HEIR APPARENT

BY DAVID IVES

ADAPTED FROM
LE LÉGATAIRE UNIVERSEL
BY JEAN-FRANÇOIS REGNARD

★

DRAMATISTS
PLAY SERVICE
INC.

This play is for Michael Kahn,
in gratitude and admiration,
and because it made him laugh.

AUTHOR'S NOTE
or: Meeting Monsieur Regnard

Voltaire said, "Whoever doesn't enjoy Regnard doesn't deserve to admire Molière."

Now there's a puff line to put on a theatre marquee.

Consider these tidbits from the life of Jean-François Regnard: First, that as your average young man of twenty-three gadding about the world, he was taken prisoner in 1778 by Algerian pirates; sold into slavery; did six months' hard labor; got ransomed; and when he arrived home hung his slave-chains on the wall in his Paris house. Second, that after a cushy Treasury job, he launched himself as a comic playwright at age thirty-eight and became the Next Big Thing after Molière. Third, that after he'd been buried one hundred and twenty-five years, some kids found his skeleton when his local church was being renovated, and the kids used his skull as a projectile.

In other words, Regnard had an archetypal career as a playwright: a slave while alive, a football when dead.

Add to this that he was loved by all who knew him; that he made a great portion of his fortune on a gambling spree (he wrote a fine play called *The Gambler*); and that, passing through Lapland, he caused a furor because of his uncontrollable laughter at a typical Lapp funeral. His name is cognate with *renard*, the French word for fox, and he lived up to it. "*Il faut par notre esprit faire notre destin,*" Crispin says in *The Heir Apparent*. "It's with our wits that we create our fates."

The buoyancy with which Regnard lived is so intrinsic to his art that the man and his work are one. The play at hand (from 1708, titled *Le Légataire universel*) is worldly, utterly honest, satirical without being condemnatory, often bawdy, sometimes scatological, now and then macabre, and it craves jokes as a drunkard craves his liquor. Like a drunkard, the play will do anything to find the liquor, as Regnard goes off on knockabout detours hunting for laughs — not out of desperation but out of brio. Granted, some of *Heir* is a shameless rip-off of Molière's *Imaginary Invalid*. But is there anything in *Le Malade imaginaire* to match the servant Crispin's inspired impersonations?

4

Because Regnard was writing as French classical theatre was heading into a century of much different character, the verse dialogue is more conversational than Molière's, the concerns more bourgeois, while the farce is turned up (as they say in *Spinal Tap*) all the way to eleven. One can draw a straight line from *Légataire* to Feydeau's middle-class nightmares, and straight from there, or should I say down from there, to TV sitcoms. And what could be more up-to-date than his characters' almost feral obsession with money?

When Michael Kahn sent me *Le Légataire universel* to look at for possible adaptation for D.C.'s Shakespeare Theatre Company, I had never heard of Regnard. Yet, just as when Michael had sent me Corneille's *Le Menteur* two years previously (which became *The Liar*, which became Michael's priceless production, which turned out to be the most fun I ever had working on any play) I needed only a single reading to know that I had to take on the piece. The off-color jokes made me howl even while I marveled at Regnard's facility at rendering them in graceful yet conversational couplets.

The original Washington production (God bless Michael Kahn!) had a pig in it. I mean, an actual pig onstage. For the New York production at Classic Stage Company, brilliantly directed by John Rando, I cut the pig and made a number of other revisions here and there, as time had taught me where the play needed tightening and/or embellishment. I also learned immensely from Carson Elrod, the comic genius who played Crispin to perfection in both productions.

How to bring the play into English? I took it as my job, while pruning some of his more extravagant asides, to mirror Regnard's restless inventiveness and tumbling action. As with *The Liar*, I took my liberties. Among other things, I beefed up Isabelle and Madame Argante, both of whom disappear in the original for the bulk of the play. Geronte held such delicious comic possibilities I probably almost doubled his part. I extended the Geronte-versus-Eraste marriage complication and embellished the impersonations that are the play's set pieces. Finally I attempted a more satisfying ending, since the original — like many French plays of that period — simply stops, abruptly, just when we expect a final cascade of unravelings and recognitions.

Working with (I won't say "on") Regnard has been a delight, for he's been, as he was in life, the best of company. As Lady Mary Wortley Montagu said of Henry Fielding: "It is a pity he was not immortal, he was so formed for happiness." Wouldn't it be wonderful if Regnard could be raised from his tomb — not to be a genial, cranial plaything this time, but to take his rightful place in the English-speaking theatre as a master of comedy, for gaiety ran in his veins as his birthright.

"Les gens d'esprit n'ont point besoin de précepteur," says Crispin in a line I didn't include. "True wits don't need a tutor." In that sense, Regnard was a natural.

THE HEIR APPARENT was first performed by Shakespeare Theatre Company (Michael Kahn, Artistic Director; Chris Jenning, Managing Director) at the Lansburgh Theatre in Washington, D.C., where it opened on September 11, 2011. It was directed by Michael Kahn; the set design was by Alexander Dodge; the costume design was by Murell Horton; the lighting design was by Philip Rosenberg; the sound design was by Christopher Baine; and the original music was by Adam Wernick. The cast was as follows:

ERASTE . . . . Andrew Veenstra
ISABELLE . . . . Meg Chambers Steedle
CRISPIN . . . . Carson Elrod
LISETTE . . . . Kelly Hutchinson
GERONTE . . . . Floyd King
MADAME ARGANTE . . . . Nancy Robinette
SCRUPLE . . . . Clark Middleton

THE HEIR APPARENT, with revisions incorporated in this edition, was subsequently produced in New York City by Classic Stage Company (Brian Kulick, Artistic Director; Jeff Griffin, Managing Director), opening on April 9, 2014. It was directed by John Rando; the set design was by John Lee Beatty; the costume design was by David C. Woolard; the lighting design was by Japhy Weideman; and the sound design was by Nevin Steinberg of Acme Sound Partners. The cast was as follows:

ERASTE . . . . Dave Quay
ISABELLE . . . . Amelia Pedlow
CRISPIN . . . . Carson Elrod
LISETTE . . . . Claire Karpen
GERONTE . . . . Paxton Whitehead
MADAME ARGANTE . . . . Suzanne Bertish
SCRUPLE . . . . David Pittu

CHARACTERS

(in order of speaking)

ERASTE ("uh-RAST"), our young hero, in love with:

ISABELLE ("IZ-uh-bel"), our charming and beautiful heroine.

CRISPIN ("kree-SPAN"), a crafty young manservant, in love with:

LISETTE ("lee-ZET"), a down-to-earth maid.

GERONTE ("zhur-AUNT"), miserly old uncle to Eraste.

MADAME ARGANTE ("ar-GAUNT"), Isabelle's dowager mother.

SCRUPLE, a lawyer who is very, very *small*.

PLACE

Paris, the house of Geronte.

TIME

Spring 1708.

NOTES

"Madam" spelled *without* an "e" is pronounced "MAD-um."
"Madame" *with* an "e" is pronounced "muh-DAM."

"Eulalie" is pronounced "YOO-luh-lee."

THE HEIR APPARENT

ACT ONE

Paris, 1708. The parlor in Geronte's house. A spring morning. A door at right to the rest of the house and doors up center toward a foyer. A window, left, with curtains and shutters. A large thronelike armchair. Some bottles and glasses filled with colored liquids. On shelves, decades of accumulated stuff. Prominent are "The Box," an ornamental chest chained to an altar-like pedestal, and a tall and odd-looking clock. The clock whirs and chimes with a strange, agitated farting noise. Lisette enters from right and throws open the curtains and shutters.

CRISPIN. *(Offstage.)*
    Lisette…?
(Crispin enters from center, breathless.)
    Lisette…!
LISETTE.
             What's up, Crispin?
CRISPIN. *(Embracing her.)*
                     My energizer!
LISETTE.
    Well, well. Since when are you an early riser?
CRISPIN.
    Since working for the nephew to your miser
    And there is hell to pay today, my pet.
    The old man hasn't kicked the bucket yet…?
    Geronte's alive? Please say he isn't dead!
LISETTE.
    If you can call it life, he's out of bed.
    So yes, alive and hoarding breaths like francs.

CRISPIN.

    I know I never pray, but — God? My thanks!

LISETTE.

    Well, God nor gold will help the old man thrive.

    I thought last night would be his last alive.

    Twenty-two times he fell into a swoon

    And lay as limply as a pitted prune.

    He only lived thanks to these brews I craft.

CRISPIN. *(Picks up one of the bottles.)*

    Your über-laxative? That healing draft?

LISETTE.

    I irrigated him both fore and aft.

    He popped up blinking, did a quick pavane,

    And hopped a polka to the closest john.

CRISPIN.

    Ironic talent, making dead men dance.

LISETTE.

    I'm high colonic mistress of all France.

    But what's this interest in the old man's health?

CRISPIN.

    My master's urgent need for all his wealth.

    The gold is safe?

LISETTE. *(Indicates The Box.)*

                        Locked in its air-tight chest.

CRISPIN.

    With luck, my master's well-deserved bequest.

LISETTE.

    Dream on, Crispin. With nephews thick as flies?

    Who each would rob, maim, kill, or pulverize

    To get your master's piece of the estate?

CRISPIN.

    Yeah, but Eraste's this money's proper mate!

    And not just 'cuz he's up to here in bills.

    There's now *Madame Argante.*

LISETTE.

                      I'm getting chills.

CRISPIN.

    Two years he's pledged in stealth to Isabelle?

    Last night, Eraste decides it's time to tell.

    What happens but her dragon-headed mom,

The dread Madame Argante, explodes *this* bomb:
Unless Eraste is named Geronte's lone heir,
I mean *sole, solitary, single* heir,
Isabelle's history and Eraste can rot.
How'll you and I afford to tie the knot?
How'll we run off to sunny Mandalay?
LISETTE.
Then say some prayers. He makes his will *today*.
And would you like to hear how deep's his greed?
To save on writing up this crucial deed,
He hired a lawyer no taller than a creeper,
As if — because he's short? — he might come cheaper.
But wait a sec ... she's here!
CRISPIN.
                                 Madame Argante?
LISETTE.
Since sunrise she's been holed up with Geronte.
They locked the door and blocked it with a chair
But just "by chance" I *did* hear ...
CRISPIN.
                                           Yes?
LISETTE.
                                    "Sole heir."
Plus lots of talk of wills and deeds and money —
With Isabelle's name neck-and-neck.
CRISPIN.
                                     Oh, *honey*!
You don't know what that means? Farewell to dread!
They're raining money on my master's head!
(Eraste enters from center. A noose hangs around his neck.)
ERASTE.
My friends — no, please don't try to cheer me up.
All night I drank of sorrow's weary cup,
Tempted by poison, gunshot, and the rope.
(Shows the noose's label.)
The cheapest noose they had. The brand-name? *"Hope."*
CRISPIN.
Roll up your clothesline, sir. Prepare to marry.
Madame Argante's in there.

11

ERASTE.

So?

CRISPIN.

Cash and carry!
Why would your uncle hang with such a pill —
Unless to craft a wedding deed-slash-will?

ERASTE.

You mean I'll get to marry Isabella?

CRISPIN.

Today you're Paris's most happy fella!

ERASTE.

So we'll be one?!
(Lets out a celebratory howl.)

CRISPIN.

Yeah, hey, the wedding's bliss,
But — Isabelle aside? — you'll have all *this*.
And stocks ... and bonds ...

ERASTE.

... and gold ...

CRISPIN.

... the plate, the crest ...

ERASTE.

That ugly clock, this ornamental chest ...
He'll settle all on me...?

CRISPIN.

You wanna bet?

ERASTE. *(Collapsing into Crispin's arms.)*

Crispin, my heart!

CRISPIN.

Hang on. You can't die yet.
Wait till you're solvent, in a gold pavilion.

LISETTE.

Riding through Paris on a silver pillion.

ERASTE.

Why not? The old man's worth *an easy MILLION!*

CRISPIN, ERASTE, and LISETTE.

A million! A million! A million!

ERASTE.

Thank God! Since each day's mail brings some new threat.
(Takes out some letters.)

"Monsieur, I'll throw you into jail for debt."
Or this: "Your date with the Bastille is nigh."
But Uncle's will could put them off me. Why?

CRISPIN, ERASTE, and LISETTE.

A million! A million! A million!

ERASTE.

But wait. What if this whole deal comes unsprung?
Some hitch, some cog, some tiny cam, or camlet?
You know my uncle. What if ...

CRISPIN.

Hey. *Prince Hamlet.*

The Battleaxe is in there on your side.
You got a Cadillac to smooth your ride.

(Madame Argante enters from right, unnoticed by Eraste.)

ERASTE.

You're right. He hasn't got a snowball's chance.
She'll turn him into stone with one chill glance!
This *is* the basilisk, Madame Argante!
She whom the Prince of Darkness couldn't daunt.
She next to whom a rock looks nonchalant.
Who makes Godzilla seem a mad bacchante.
To whom Attila is a dilettante.
She who ...

MADAME ARGANTE.

Monsieur Eraste.

ERASTE.

Madame Argante.

MADAME ARGANTE.

I know what you want. Words that might unmuddy
What I've been up to in your uncle's study,
An explication of our tête-à-tête.
You love my daughter, don't you? Better yet,
You crave at any cost her satisfaction?

ERASTE.

Oh, madam, I would brave Ulysses' action!
To win her bliss I'd ape Achilles' test!
Great Vulcan's flame ...

MADAME ARGANTE.

Sir, lay this noise to rest,
And more important don't intone to me

Names each of which is quite unknown to me.
Your friend Ulysses visits which salon?
This Vulcan's not in *my* arrondissement.
ERASTE.
The only purpose of my earthly zeal
Is this: to broker an unearthly deal
And see my Isabelle to holy marriage.
All worldly riches I hereby disparage!
What are they to the treasures in her look?
MADAME ARGANTE.
Such ardor is so precious — in a book.
Yes, knights and mincing ladies, lovers true
Phloxes and chocolate boxes … I could spew.
No matter. I just framed in there a pact
Which leaves your every lavish dream intact
And renders you my Isabella's savior.
Don't thank me, please. You know I loathe *behavior*.
ERASTE.
But how much…?
MADAME ARGANTE.

        As I loathe being stopped when speaking.
You note this lovely wedding deed?
(Produces a paper.)

        No peeking.
Regarding love and marriage, pounds and pence
There is an art to building up suspense.
I will say this: the stocks, the bonds …
ERASTE.

        … the ancient crest?
MADAME ARGANTE.
That ugly clock, this ornamental chest …
ERASTE.
They're all included?
MADAME ARGANTE.

        In a clean account
Climaxing here
(Indicates a spot in the document, which she keeps close.)

        in an obscene amount
Set off in its own box, in bright vermillion.
I won't say what it is.

ERASTE.

A mill...?

MADAME ARGANTE.

A million.

I'm off to her and, if you don't refuse,

I'll bring Belle back to celebrate the news.

ERASTE.

Refuse, madame...?

MADAME ARGANTE.

Fine, fine. Just please don't *babble*.

LISETTE.

This way.

MADAME ARGANTE.

I'll see myself out, thank you. — *Rabble*.

(Madame Argante exits center.)

CRISPIN, ERASTE, and LISETTE.

A million! A million! A million!

LISETTE.

Congratulations, sir, from social scum!

ERASTE.

Bless you, Lisette.

CRISPIN.

I hope you'll fling a crumb

The *rabble*'s way when once you're in your palace.

ERASTE.

Crispin, I'll be a font. A brimming chalice.

A bottle ever tipped to pour a toast.

I'll pass out lucre like a priest the Host!

CRISPIN.

You'll front me dough so I can wed my crony?

ERASTE.

And rent the Pope to head the ceremony.

LISETTE.

Perhaps I could be maid to your fair dame?

ERASTE.

And paid in pearls. But have I lost all shame?

While sniffing francs like some fine muscatel

I utterly forgot my Isabelle!

Who glows with rays bright Aphrodite speckles!

CRISPIN.

And who you'll lose if you don't get these shekels.

'Cuz don't forget, you still don't own the till.

Not till your uncle writes and signs a will.

So keep him stoked. A hundred things could screw this.

LISETTE.

A lawyer's on his way here to pursue this

And since he's late, Crispin, go fetch him, pronto.

CRISPIN.

Aye, aye, commander.

(To Eraste, à la The Lone Ranger.)

Kemo sabe!

ERASTE. *(Ditto.)*

Tonto!

CRISPIN.

Wait, where's this lawyer, what's his name again?

LISETTE.

You cannot miss the guy. He's two-foot-ten.

Around the corner, by the name of Scruple.

CRISPIN.

How droll. A lawyer no bigger than a loophole.

I'm gone!

(Crispin exits center.)

LISETTE.

He's right, sir. Till this will is signed

You have to keep your uncle's mind inclined.

What with his moods, we don't want some kerfuffle.

ERASTE.

Today my uncle's fur shall go unruffled.

My sole intent will be to acquiesce,

My every syllable some form of "*yes*."

LISETTE.

I hope it works.

GERONTE. *(Offstage.)*

Lisette!

LISETTE.

He's coming, sir. God bless.

(Geronte enters from right in a shabby nightshirt and robe, leaning on a cane, hacking and coughing. He wears a tight cap with fur earflaps.)

GERONTE.
Good morning, nephew.
ERASTE.

Uncle — *absolutely!*

GERONTE.
I beg your pardon?
ERASTE.

Yes! As you astutely
Proclaimed: "*Good morning!*" So we're in accord!
What better good can any morn afford
Than greeting you, my luminary *unc*?
A model for us all! What spark! What spunk!
So full of ...

LISETTE.

Mucus?

ERASTE.

... life.

GERONTE.

What are you — drunk?

ERASTE.
Yes. No! Oh, please not there, sir. This is cozier.
(Leading him to the chair.)
GERONTE.
Don't touch me.
ERASTE.

There. I've never seen you rosier.

GERONTE.
No?
ERASTE.

No. Yes! I detect distinct improvement.

GERONTE.
Then you can thank the twenty stinking movements
Induced by *her* to keep me from my grave.
A stream of ordure black enough to pave
A road from Paris to the far Crimea.
ERASTE.
But otherwise, how ...
GERONTE.

Diarrhea! Diarrhea!

ERASTE.

But …

GERONTE.

> *Diarrhea!* Say it.

ERASTE.

Diarrhea …

GERONTE.

Diarrhea! After that, I should be proud?
Another night like that, just buy my shroud.
A *cheap* one. Nothing gaudy. Nothing sunny.

ERASTE.

How are you now?

GERONTE.

Who cares? How is my *money*?

Lisette!

LISETTE.

Monsieur?

GERONTE.

Investigate *The Box*!

LISETTE.

The Box is chained up fast.

GERONTE.

The Box's locks?

LISETTE.

Secure, monsieur.

GERONTE.

Now bring *The Box* to me!

LISETTE.

For that, Lord Paranoid, I'll need *The Key*.
(Geronte takes out a key fastened to an endless string around his neck. She takes it and, trailing line across the room, frees the moneybox.)

GERONTE.

For gold I deem no safeguard too extreme.
But this reminds me … Yes! I had a dream!
For taking flight last night on wings I flew
Up from my bed and over Paris, through
The air where cloudlets dangled, draped in swags —
Plump, saffron clouds all shaped like moneybags!
Beyond the sun, a glittering *Louis d'or*,
I reached the stars, a spray of silver ore

Strewn on the jeweler's velvet of the skies!
But then I knew I'd gone to paradise.
For lo! A road before me, lined with banks
Where I was reunited with ...
ERASTE.

Your wife?

GERONTE.

My francs.

(Lisette hands him The Box, and he hugs it.)
My first centime! Oh, happy, trusty chest!
(Gives The Box back to Lisette, who re-secures it while he hacks and coughs.)
ERASTE.
But sir, these ills of yours must be addressed!
GERONTE.
You mean buy pills? And pile up bills from docs?
Don't you know what's important, boy?
ERASTE.

The Box?

GERONTE.

The Box!

Some quack should charge ten sous to stoke my gut?
Two francs to poke a plunger up my butt?
It's criminal! Extortion past endurance!
Of course, if we had national health insurance ...
But this is seventeen-oh-what?
ERASTE.

Oh-eight.

GERONTE.
I wouldn't pay for it at any rate!
I'd rather bid the Reaper come and visit —
And if he had a ring I'd kneel and kiss it!
ERASTE.
And so would I!
(With a cry, Geronte slumps over the arm of his chair, still.)

But — Uncle? Sir? What is it?

Lisette, what is this? One of his attacks?
LISETTE.
It *was* one.
ERASTE.

So he's dead?

LISETTE.

Relax. Relax.

GERONTE. *(Sitting back up. During this, Crispin enters.)*
I thought I saw a coin between those cracks.
But boy, you greet me on a special day.
Where is this lawyer? Lisette?

LISETTE.

Crispin?

CRISPIN.

He's on his way.

ERASTE. *("Innocent.")*
But why do you need a lawyer?

GERONTE.

To write my will.

ERASTE.
Oh, sir, don't even say the word! A chill
Runs through me at the sound. The thought's appalling!
"Testament." "Legacy." Each word recalling
The passing of the dearest man alive.

GERONTE.
Who?

ERASTE.

You. Whose death I doubt I could survive.

GERONTE.
I feel the same, but we're both sentimental.

ERASTE.
Of course, a will is good, it's fundamental.

GERONTE.
Yes — given the sharks who're circling me like chum.

ERASTE.
You don't mean...?

GERONTE.

Fortune-hunters!

ERASTE.

Sir, I'm *dumb*!
There're parasites who're chasing for your gold?
Your stocks, your bonds, the real estate you hold,
Your tapestries, your plate, your ancient crest,
That ugly clock, this ornamental chest...?

GERONTE.

Have you had all my property assessed?

ERASTE.

    Yes. No! But when you pen your final sentiments
    Let not my love for you be an impediment
    To anything you plan to leave, or settle.
    My feelings for you need no precious metal.

GERONTE.

    You're good to me, my boy. You're ...

ERASTE.

                                   Heaven-sent?

GERONTE.

    And since you're here, I'll tell you my intent.
    I'm going to name one individual
    Who'll get it all. The full residual.

ERASTE.

    One person, Uncle? I don't mean to quiz ...

GERONTE.

    Oh, I know who that special person is.

(Taking Eraste's hand.)

    One close to me, with power to love and please.
    That person I shall leave, for life, at ease —
    With francs that dance a solid gold cotillion!
    Do you know what I'm worth?

CRISPIN, ERASTE, and LISETTE.

                             A mill...?

GERONTE.

                                 A million.

    Think that's enough to fund a happy life?
    A sum sufficient to support ... *a wife?*

ERASTE. *(Kissing Geronte's hand.)*

    I love you, sir. I love you! That's my story.
    I don't ask much. A small memento mori.
    Just ten centimes, to think on you and hold —
    A souvenir of you, to thwart the cold.

GERONTE.

    You disagree?

ERASTE.

        No!

GERONTE.

                    Find my plan too dire?
ERASTE.

Of course, you have to do as you desire.
The larger family, though, might feel some ire ...
GERONTE.

They wish me nothing and I'll parrot them.
I'll leave them zip! I'll disinherit them!
ERASTE.

Oh, sir, you have to leave them *something*. Do!
It's simple human charity.
GERONTE.

                            Not a sou!
These money-sniffing dogs, all preened and oiled,
What better pleasure than to see them foiled?
To see it, I'd float down off my heavenly cloud.
LISETTE.

Unless you're roasting with a toastier crowd.
(Offstage knocking.)
GERONTE.

Ah, there's Madame Argante and her coquette.
Let them in. First, though, my best wig, Lisette.
LISETTE.

"Best wig," monsieur? That thing's more like a pet.
God knows what animals hooked up to breed it.
You shouldn't put it on, sir. You should feed it.
GERONTE.

I'll wear my hair no matter how you jig —
And swear I'll wear it, missy, in my wig.
LISETTE.

Well, I'll swear, too, and it's no perjury:
What *you* need's drastic plastic surgery.
ERASTE.

Enough, Lisette. You're torturing the man.
GERONTE.

I'll fetch my wig myself.
LISETTE.

                            It's in the can,
Next to your girlie mags.

GERONTE.

You're venomous!

And not one word to them about my enemas!

(Geronte exits right.)

CRISPIN, ERASTE, and LISETTE.

A million…! A million…! A million…!

(Lisette exits center to answer the front door.)

ERASTE.

The virtues of agreeability!

Forget to-be-or-not-to-be-ity.

Suck up! Eat crow! That's all one has to do.

CRISPIN.

To thine own pocket — sorry, *self* — be true.

ERASTE.

Now where's this lawyer?

CRISPIN.

He'll be here any sec.

Or rather — *shortly*, since the man's a speck.

(Isabelle runs in from center, embracing Eraste.)

ISABELLE.

Darling!

ERASTE.

Oh, Isabelle!

ISABELLE.

So how's it *going*?

What do you think our chances are?

ERASTE.

They're glowing!

My uncle's like some madcap, lavish aunt.

ISABELLE.

We'll get enough to wed?

ERASTE.

Enough to flaunt!

He's going to leave it all … Madame Argante.

(Madame Argante has entered from center with Lisette.)

MADAME ARGANTE.

Good day again, Monsieur Eraste …

(Noting Crispin.)

… and so on.

ERASTE.

A joyful day, by what I have to go on.

MADAME ARGANTE.

Yet sad, the settling of a patrimony.

And then to think of adding matrimony!

ERASTE.

How could a marriage our gladsome spirits douse?

MADAME ARGANTE.

You wouldn't say that if you'd known my spouse.

That pillar of the church, that foe of whoredom,

That undisputed lord of bedroom boredom.

(Eraste and Isabella clinch and kiss.)

STOP THAT.

(Geronte reenters in a fluffy wig with his earflapped cap over it.)

GERONTE.

Madame Argante, forgive my tardiness.

My maid's too-typical foolhardiness

Arrested me in grooming for our chat.

LISETTE.

Monsieur, there's something nesting in your hat.

GERONTE.

Welcome, Georgina, to my humble cell.

ISABELLE.

If you mean me, sir, my name's Isabelle.

I understand you passed a doubtful night?

GERONTE.

Mere gossip, mademoiselle, from ghouls who'd fright

Me prematurely to my grave to rot.

I *did* make twenty stinking visits to *The Pot.*

A stream of ordure ...

ERASTE.

                              Uncle? Bad idea.

GERONTE.

You're right. It's wrong to mention diarrhea.

A *stream of ordure's* hardly social grist.

LISETTE.

And enemas are strictly off the list.

GERONTE.

They are! We will not enter that morass.

As for my piles ...

ERASTE.
                              I think we'll let that pass.
    Where were we in our beatific meeting?
GERONTE.
    Just don't believe the lying, thieving, cheating
    Hucksters who'd have you think me at
(Coughs, spits.)
                                        death's door.
ISABELLE.
    You, sir? Life's living, breathing metaphor?
GERONTE.
    That's what I am! No thanks to those piranha
    Who'd grab my gold through drams of belladonna.
ERASTE.
    But, Uncle, no one here wants to deprive you.
    And see, you've this madonna to revive you!
    One glance from whom is like a waking kiss.
GERONTE.
    I've noticed how you gaze on this young miss.
    Ah, pungent funk of feminine attraction!
    The girl's beguiling, is she?
ERASTE.
                              To distraction.
    Praising her wildly would comprise detraction.
GERONTE.
    She has the stuff to bless a husband's house?
ERASTE.
    With every virtue of a perfect spouse.
    Beauty to burn. Unmatched intelligence.
    An ideal fit of wit and elegance.
GERONTE.
    She's young.
ERASTE.
                Her age presents no barrier.
GERONTE.
    Who wouldn't grasp this lass?
ERASTE.
                              And like a terrier.
GERONTE.
    One needs substantial means to carry her.

ERASTE.

    She's like the Nile. She's rich without a source!
    She's fire and light! An elemental force!
    Yet strong as oak. No wind or change can vary her.
    I love her!

GERONTE.

               Good. I'm going to marry her.

ISABELLE, CRISPIN, ERASTE, and LISETTE.

    You *what*?!

GERONTE.

          I said I'm going to marry her.
    At three o'clock this afternoon.
(To Isabelle.)

                    My saint!

ISABELLE.

    If you'll excuse me, all, I'm going to faint.
(She does so, into Eraste's arms.)

GERONTE.

    Poor girl. No doubt the rapture was too strong.

ISABELLE. *(Waking immediately.)*

    I fainted, sir, because this plan is wrong.
    We — *wed*?

GERONTE.

        Today at three.

ISABELLE.

               You've lost a screw!

GERONTE.

    Yes, I agree. Let's move it up to two.
    Oh, kitten…!

ISABELLE.

      Kitten?

GERONTE.

            See how like two pills
    Your brilliant eyes have remedied my ills,
    Your smoothing curves my soothing anesthetic!

ISABELLE.

    My body, sir, is not your paramedic.

GERONTE.

    You're my elixir! Promising a cure
    Stronger than Bromo-Seltzer — and more sure.

I have no doubt, thanks to your healing syrups
I'll soon be back inside the manly stirrups,
Erect upon the saddle, hot to trot,
And in nine months we'll see a screaming tot.
My features, naturally. Mouth, lyrical ...
LISETTE.
This babe would also be a miracle.
For pardon, sir, but you, who're plugged with phlegm,
Whose every cough proclaims a requiem,
With stones to pass, a bloated spleen, a limp,
With gas enough to float a German blimp,
You who're asthmatic, rheumatic, and myopic,
Smegmatic, aspermatic, misanthropic,
Sclerotic, cirrhotic, phlebotic,
Thrombotic, neurotic, necrotic,
You'd put on gloves and spats and play the groom
Who need but one small leap to reach the tomb?
GERONTE.
I gather that you somehow disapprove?
LISETTE.
Your bowels are the only parts that move!
GERONTE.
I let her fling these barbs designed to slay me.
LISETTE.
Yeah, free speech being the only thing you *pay* me.
Monsieur, if Satan's tempted you to wed
Pick someone apropos — like someone *dead.*
Leave her a guy who doesn't buy his hair.
About this tall, brown eyes, quite debonair,
A hundred fifty pounds and tightly assed —
Someone remarkably like young Eraste.
GERONTE.
Eraste?
LISETTE.
              Eraste.
GERONTE.
                        What's he to my Georgina?
I know my needs.
LISETTE.
                        A bowl of hot farina?

27

GERONTE.

A second self! A mate! That's what will mend me.
A nurse who day-in, day-out can attend me.
An aide-de-camp who'll damp my tiniest sneeze,
Empty my slops and rid my shorts of fleas,
Twenty-four-seven she'll be on her knees,
Succoring me.

ISABELLE, CRISPIN, ERASTE, and LISETTE.

WHAT?

GERONTE.

Succoring, I said.

But showing her zeal, too, in the master bed.
Why leave my gold to some finagling ferret
When I've a wife to dangle such a carrot
In front of? She who'd gladly bear the brunt of
My little moods and piddling peccadilloes,
Whose arms will wrap me like two weeping willows,
Whose hands will keep my household spick-and-span.
Who'll be all things unto a needy man!

LISETTE.

Yeah — hooker, housemaid, and prescription plan.

ERASTE.

My uncle's right.

ISABELLE.

He's what?

ERASTE.

He's an *adult.*

LISETTE.

I'll say.

ERASTE.

Who're we to jib and not exult?
Yes! I say let him marry whom he please!
Perhaps *Madame Argante*, though, disagrees…?

MADAME ARGANTE.

I? Not at all. I find this prospect thrilling.

ERASTE.

There's not *another beau*, who's right and willing?

MADAME ARGANTE.

No.

ERASTE.

> One who loves her?

MADAME ARGANTE.

> > > No.

ERASTE.

> > > Who'd kneel in thanks?

MADAME ARGANTE.

> No beau I know who has a million francs.

ERASTE.

> You asked one if he craved her satisfaction.

MADAME ARGANTE.

> And now she gets it! Why? Does this transaction
> Distress you somehow? Give you cause for pain?
> What other suitors lose is Bella's gain.
> True, gold's no substitute for love's rich spread,
> But where's the sandwich when there ain't no bread?

ERASTE.

> But sir, you said you'd name a legatee
> Who loves you.

GERONTE.

> > As Georgina here loves *me*!

> Why? Do you somehow blanch at my design?

ERASTE.

> No! Sir, your plan's infernal, it's so fine!
> You want to marry? Why should *I* feel sorry?

GERONTE.

> I'm going to leave you that memento mori.
> You know — **your** sentimental souvenir?
> Indeed, I'll leave you ten centimes *a year*!
> So there, Madame Argante. We've done our task.

ISABELLE.

> May I say something? I, who wasn't asked
> About the fitness of this wedding plot?
> Remember me? "Georgina"? Who I'm *not*?
> I, the sad puck in Mama's game of hockey?
> The lucky slave who'll fumigate your Jockeys,
> The blot put here on earth to dab your nose,
> Affix your dickey, mend your flealess clothes,
> To sport with you with "*zeal*," not grin and bear it,
> The succorer of any dangled carrot?

And let me get this straight: As for your gold
It only comes with *you*, to have and hold?
I have to buy this show or have to hike it?
Must swig your Kool-Aid any way you spike it?
Must sing your song no matter how you mike it?
Is that your quid-pro-quo?
GERONTE.

                              I knew you'd like it.
LISETTE.

Monsieur Eraste, speak for this mademoiselle!
ERASTE.

I still say Uncle's right.
LISETTE.

                       He's booked for *Hell!*
He's seventy! He's dull! He's asinine!
GERONTE.

Excuse me, please. I'm only sixty-nine.
ISABELLE.

So you advise me to go through with this?
ERASTE.

I urge you to, and wish you every bliss.
Think of liquidity. Think of expedience.
Dismiss your id. Think filial obedience.
GERONTE.

Exactly.
ERASTE.

            Swallow personal disgust.
So what if, when he urinates, it's dust?
GERONTE.

That happens.
ERASTE.

                So what, his every ailment?
GERONTE. *(Producing a long sheet of paper.)*

I've got a list of them, for your regalement.
ERASTE.

Or if he's to his hips in River Styx?
GERONTE.

It's nothing that a trip to Lourdes can't fix.

ERASTE.

The die is cast! It's destiny! It's fate!

Behold your perfect, predetermined mate!

ISABELLE.

Well, sir. You're eloquent as this man's shill.

You think that I should marry him? *I will!*

GERONTE.

I knew she would.

ISABELLE.

I'll brave those wedding choirs

If they must pry "I do" from me with pliers!

MADAME ARGANTE.

See there? Give her a task, she'll never shirk.

GERONTE.

But I sense Mother Nature hard at work.

Digestive tract, you know. I'm off to stool!

(Geronte exits right.)

LISETTE.

Behold the bottom of the dating pool.

And sir, you'd leave your filly to this fool?

MADAME ARGANTE.

Come, daughter.

ERASTE.

No, madame, with all due deference,

Did you not swear to me I'd be your preference?

Did you not promise me your daughter's hand?

MADAME ARGANTE.

Provided you provided gold and land.

Is it my fault your spending powers are spent?

That you're one of the Ninety-Nine Percent?

Rejoice! The gold and land are Isabella's!

ERASTE.

By wedding *him?*

MADAME ARGANTE.

So call me overzealous.

That happens, acting on one's children's part.

I'm really just a soccer mom, at heart.

ERASTE.

You'll do this, mademoiselle, you'll be his toy?

ISABELLE.

I am amazed, monsieur, my fount of joy
By you of all the world should come in question.
Did you not bid me disregard digestion
And swallow giving *succor* to Geronte?
Filial obedience? Was that not your taunt?

ERASTE.

You missed how, on the inside, I was winking?

ISABELLE.

Your inner tic escaped me. I was blinking —
Thanks to some prickly tears that blocked my view.
Well, I have a trousseau to buy. Adieu!

(Isabelle exits center.)

ERASTE.

Madame Argante — what if I changed his mind?
Produced a will that named *me*, underlined,
Sole heir to all my uncle is possessed of?
Would you accept that as a fitting test of
My worthiness to have your daughter's hand?
Give me one day. One hour. One grain of sand
Trickling into an hourglass and I'll do it.

MADAME ARGANTE.

You have till two o'clock. But if I rue it,
This rash and most untypical compassion,
You will have fucked yourself in royal fashion.

(Madame Argante exits.)

ERASTE.

Okay, I'm ready. I'm fired up. I'm *scorchin'*!
But, Christ! How can I pull this off? Cruel Fortune
Wants me a gerbil puffing on its wheel.
Fortune — which kicks its gate and turns its heel,
Slamming the door on opportunity.

CRISPIN.

So slam it back, and with impunity!
Don't give me Fortune's wheel and Fortune's gates —
It's with our wits that we create our fates.
So va fungoo the Unforeseeable!
And hey, nice job there, bein' agreeable.

ERASTE.

Some drops of oil to grease a squeaky strut!

CRISPIN.

There's lubrication, sir, and kissing butt.

ERASTE.

You're right, Crispin. To truckle is to suck.

LISETTE.

He's coming back.

CRISPIN.

Be firm.

ERASTE.

I will.

LISETTE.

Good luck.

(Geronte reenters.)

GERONTE.

Well, that was certainly inopportune,

All to eject one small black macaroon.

LISETTE.

Thank you for that.

GERONTE.

My guests, they showed no pique?

LISETTE.

No, you might say they turned the *other* cheek.

I have to tell you, not to be a smarty,

That was one hell of an engagement party.

GERONTE.

A party! Yes — that puts in mind, Lisette,

We'll need some kind of festive marriage fête.

But nothing too expensive. Nothing gaudy.

ERASTE.

An undertaker to collect the body?

GERONTE.

Musicians — half a score or so, or nice.

Or six, or three. A soloist is fine.

What player comes cheap who's worthy of my wife?

LISETTE.

A flatulist who blows a penny fife?

GERONTE.

Good, good. And food. But simple, off the cuff.

LISETTE.

A bean sucked off our sleeve, is that enough?

GERONTE.

I'll pay one franc. Anything more is thieving.

LISETTE.

Great. Where's the franc?

(Geronte takes out a purse, takes a purse out of the purse, takes a purse out of that purse, and tries to pry a coin out of its depths.)

GERONTE.

Right here. Right here. Right here ...

(Weeps.)

LISETTE.

Monsieur, stop *grieving!*

ERASTE.

No! I say it's absurd! It's creepy! Sick!

GERONTE.

I beg your pardon?

ERASTE.

What a filthy trick!

GERONTE.

You seem upset.

ERASTE.

Oh, DO I?

GERONTE.

With what cause?

ERASTE.

The way you'd flout both God's and Nature's laws
By wedding while you're in the Reaper's jaws!
And then to think of generating tots
When your machinery lacks the jigawatts?
It's ludicrous. It's humorous. It's sad.
And by a woman *whom I love*, I'd add,
And who requites me in that sentiment.
What you need, sir, 's a Final Testament.
Wed pen to paper. Copulate with ink.
Beget a will. I'll say it, I won't blink.
Will will will WILL. And under "legatee"?
A single sentence designating ME.
The race goes to the fit? I'm here for christening!
Well, Uncle?

GERONTE.

                             Sorry, lad, I wasn't listening.

About this wedding ...

ERASTE.

                                Sir, I must protest.

Do I not rate at least a small bequest?

GERONTE.

Yes, that reminds me — I've two relatives

Who both need economic lenitives.

ERASTE.

You mean a legacy?

GERONTE.

                         They're of my breed.

ERASTE.

You said you'd not support these buzzards' greed!

Don't you detect a huge disparity?

GERONTE.

But as you say — it's simple human charity.

First, there's a nephew starving in New York,

Second, a widowed niece who married pork —

She wed the Count Cochon, pig-breeder fine

Who lent a true nobility to swine.

They'll get, as members of our family's flanks,

A small memento. Twenty thousand francs.

CRISPIN, ERASTE, and LISETTE.

What?!

GERONTE.

           Twenty thousand francs.

ERASTE.

                                All told?

GERONTE.

                                    Apiece.

ERASTE.

I didn't even know you *had* a niece!

GERONTE.

Nor I, until she wrote me this epistle.

(Takes out a letter.)

    "Dear sweetest Uncle Jerry. How I bristle

To think of you alone ... "

35

CRISPIN, ERASTE, and LISETTE.
(Alone?)
GERONTE.

" ... up there and ill.
I hope that you'll include me in your will.
Love, Widow Julie." Look, a paste-on piglet
That wags its curly pig-tail when you wiggle it.
(Shows the wiggling piglet.)
Isn't that cute?
ERASTE.

So she gets twenty thou
For sticking on a picture of a sow?
And I don't get enough to buy a loin?
GERONTE.
"P.S., I thought you'd like this shiny coin."
(Shows the coin and kisses it.)
Sweet Julie.
ERASTE.

Well, then, hell, I'll give you two!
And wiggle like a whole damn petting zoo!
GERONTE.
Nephew, this is unkind! How can you think this?
ERASTE.
How? Twenty thousand francs is how!
LISETTE. *(Gives Geronte a glass.)*

Drink this.
GERONTE.
I'm strewing gifts! For this I get a dig?
(Drains the contents of the glass.)
ERASTE.
She sent you half a sou and Porky Pig!
GERONTE.
This niece and nephew need some leverage.
So I ... Lisette — Lisette, what was that beverage...?
My guts are a volcano hotting up!
LISETTE.
I call that cocktail *Drano*. Bottoms up!
(Geronte exits right, fast.)
Well, now that we're alone, thanks to my brew,
What — short of turning Buddhist — do we do?

ERASTE.

I tried aggressiveness, I tried détente …

CRISPIN.

Try *brain power* — something lacking in Geronte.

First thing, we get back what has been bereft you

From Widow Porkfat and this New York nephew.

ERASTE.

Crispin, he'll never budge. You saw him bust me.

CRISPIN.

When he comes back, just keep him stalled — and trust me.

For this day is the Feast of St. Crispin!

Once more unto the breach! *I have a plan!*

(Starts out, but comes right back. To us.)

Okay, so do we understand the plot?

The will, Madame Argante, the wedding knot?

You got all that? Good.

(To a couple in the audience.)

You two look confused.

Let's backtrack, just to keep us all enthused.

Do you remember how, a couple times

(Amidst our author's brilliant, supple rhymes),

Geronte spoke of a New York nephew? Yes?

A widowed niece who's raising pigs, no less?

He wants to leave them money. Did you cop that?

Well, we three needy bastards need to stop that

And I might save us from the frying pan —

For this day is the Feast of St. Crispin!

Once more unto the breach! *I have a plan!*

(Crispin exits center as Isabelle runs in from there and embraces Eraste.)

ISABELLE.

Oh, darling!

ERASTE.

Love!

ISABELLE.

Forgive me, if you can.

ERASTE.

No, me.

ISABELLE.

No, me.

ERASTE.

             No, me.

ISABELLE.

                 No, me.

ERASTE.

                      Enough. We have a glitch.

ISABELLE.

Besides not marrying or being rich?

ERASTE.

He's leaving twenty thousand francs apiece
To a Yankee nephew and some fleecing niece.

ISABELLE.

I'll massacre the bitch!

LISETTE.

                Call off your dogs.

Miss Julie's in the country, raising hogs.

ISABELLE.

Can't one of us devise some brilliant plan?

LISETTE.

One of us has. Resilient, wise Crispin.

ISABELLE.

We're out of danger?

ERASTE.

               If this plan pans out.

ISABELLE.

We'll need a backup plan, to ban all doubt.
Something with all its "T"s crossed, all "I"s dotted.

ERASTE.

Something ingenious …

LISETTE.

              Something sly …

ISABELLE.

                      I've got it!

I've just had what the French call a *trouvaille*!
But wait a sec. I *am* French!

ERASTE.

             So am I!

ISABELLE and ERASTE. *(Abruptly in a French film.)*
Ah, mon amour!

ISABELLE.

> *Je t'aime!*

ERASTE.

> *Je t'aime!*

ISABELLE.

> *La lune!*

ERASTE.

> *Le soir!*

ISABELLE.
Mais quoi?
ERASTE.

> *Mais toi!*

ISABELLE.

> *Tu m'aimes?*

ERASTE.

> *Quand même!*

ISABELLE.

> *Au 'voir!*

LISETTE. *(Sobbing.)*
(So beautiful.)
(Isabelle runs out center as Geronte reenters from right.)
GERONTE.
That was a filthy trick on your employer.
Now where's my tardy teensy-weensy lawyer?
ERASTE. *(Improvising.)*
He ... said ... he had ... some documents ... to ... skim ...
GERONTE.
Fine! He won't come to me, I'll go to him.
(Starts out.)
ERASTE.
No! Uncle!
GERONTE.

> Well? What is it? What's the matter?

ERASTE.
You can't.
GERONTE.

> Can't what?

ERASTE.

> Can't visit him. An adder!

They found an adder in his attic.

GERONTE.

What?!

ERASTE.

A spitting cobra. Sounds dramatic, but
I saw the beast myself. As thick as this.
It had these two long fangs, and did it hiss!
You should've seen that python writhe and rankle.
It bit me, too.

GERONTE.

It bit you?

ERASTE.

On the ankle.
I'm feeling it, Lisette! The poison's working!

LISETTE.

Don't panic, sir! Not yet!

ERASTE.

See that? That jerking?

GERONTE.

Help him, Lisette!

LISETTE.

I can't without the ... stuff ...

ERASTE.

The anecdote.

LISETTE.

The *antidote*.

ERASTE.

It's tough —
I mean, to die without a legacy ...

GERONTE.

Poor lad.

ERASTE.

I say, *without a legacy*.

GERONTE.

What's dying like?

ERASTE.

Dying? It's like ... Tennessee ...

GERONTE.

What? Tennessee?

ERASTE. *("Delirious.")*

Tennessee! Tennessee!

40

LISETTE.
Stand back, sir. Tennessee means curtains.
GERONTE.

Shocking!
ERASTE.
Is that you, Mama? Holding me and rocking?
But what's this river? What's this darkling shore?
Dear God...!
(Offstage knocking, loud. Suddenly calm.)
Is someone knocking at the door?
(Lisette runs out center. Eraste springs to his feet.)
I feel much better now. Just lost my poise.
GERONTE. *(Hears shouting offstage.)*
But what the devil's all that bloody noise?
(Crispin enters from center, dressed as an American backwoodsman, with a drooping moustache and carrying a blunderbuss. On his head, he wears a stuffed dog. Lisette follows him in.)
CRISPIN/AMERICAN.
Aloha from New York!
GERONTE.

New York?
CRISPIN/AMERICAN. *(Ignoring Geronte; only to Eraste until noted.)*
Buon giorno!
Is this here Paris, home to whores 'n' porno?
GERONTE.
Good God.
CRISPIN/AMERICAN.
Jeez, I been poundin' on yer portal
Fer a month o' Sundees! Wondered if a mortal
Man, dawg, or woman were alive in here!
Don't smell like it. That is some atmosphere
You folks got in Paree. Whoo-*ee*, that's funky!
Stinks like the backside off a rhesus monkey.
Yer hand, sir! Je sweez on-shitt*ay*. Beau-coo!
(It's me! Crispin.)
ERASTE.
(I thought it might be you.)
CRISPIN/AMERICAN.
You don't smell that? It's downright homicidal.
Did one Ga-*ront* live at this domicidal?

GERONTE.

I am Geronte.

CRISPIN/AMERICAN.

Well, Unkie, hush my snoot!
I thought I'd find you in a funeral suit
Wrapped up and ready fer yer trip to Jesus!
Put 'er there, boy!

(Pumps Geronte's hand till further noted.)

I'm sorry 'bout the "rhesus."
Just shootin' off my trap as I will do.

GERONTE.

Monsieur, who *are* you?

CRISPIN/AMERICAN.

What's that?

GERONTE.

Who are *you?*

CRISPIN/AMERICAN.

Guess it's no mystery, you cain't place my mug.
We never met before! Gimme a hug.

GERONTE. *(Pulling away.)*

Get off of me! Explain yourself, you varlet!

CRISPIN/AMERICAN. *(Leveling his blunderbuss.)*

Them's fightin' words and you would now be scarlet.
I'd blast ya if my maw were not *yer sister.*

GERONTE.

My sister? You?

CRISPIN/AMERICAN.

I'm not yer sister, mister.
My *mother* were yer sister. I'm her kid.
A' course, she wasn't married yet. She did
Get hitched months later. Is that yer affair?
My maw's a round-heel whore? Hey, *I* don't care!

GERONTE.

This is my sister, sir, of whom you're speaking.

CRISPIN/AMERICAN.

Okay, her timing needed tweaking!

(To Lisette.)

Hi!

GERONTE.

So nephew, you came all this distance?

CRISPIN/AMERICAN. *(Leveling the blunderbuss again.)*

Why?

You doubt my word?

GERONTE.

No!

CRISPIN/AMERICAN.

You poltroon! You dastard!

I am yer nephew if I *am* a bastard,

As sure as yer a geriolatric stork.

GERONTE.

I only meant, you don't seem from New York.

CRISPIN/AMERICAN.

Oh, yer some geographic referee?

GERONTE.

I thought you might have stemmed from ... Tennessee.

ERASTE.

Tennessee! Tennessee! — Excuse me.

CRISPIN/AMERICAN.

So you got inbred idjits, too, huh. Nasty.

But hang on, you must be my cousin Rasty!

Whoa, handsome guy! I thought he'd be a mutt!

GERONTE.

One question, sir. When are you leaving?

CRISPIN/AMERICAN.

WHUT?!

Hey, I arrive here slav'rin' for your cash —

And you sit there alive and unabashed?

I am be-destitute becuz o' *you*!

So I ain't leaving till I see 'em screw

Yer coffin shut and tup it down some shaft.

As fer yer will, see here, I brung this draft

That says I get it all upon your *de*-mize.

(Produces a paper.)

Nor don't go stuffin' nothin' in yer Levi's,

'Cuz I will dig you up with my bare claws!

GERONTE.

Monsieur, had I the use of these two paws

I'd heave you out that window.

CRISPIN/AMERICAN.

Who, sir, me, sir?

GERONTE.

Yes, sir, you, sir.

CRISPIN/AMERICAN.

Haw, haw! You stupid geezer!

You cain't treat me like some vile denizen.

This here's my walls and floors and dens yer in!

It's only out the goodness o' my heart

That you ain't livin' in a shoppin' cart!

(Motions to Eraste to jump in, but Eraste doesn't understand the signal.)

So whatcha say?

(Levels the blunderbuss and cocks it loudly: CLICK!)

GERONTE.

I promise! You'll inherit!

The hour I'm gone you'll get the lot. I swear it!

CRISPIN/AMERICAN.

Okay, how long d'ya plan to be alive?

GERONTE.

I doubt I've ten days left.

CRISPIN/AMERICAN.

I'll give ya five.

Till then I'm gonna need a pide-a-terre

So me 'n' this fine pair on yer au pair

Can gnaw the prod'gal calf down to the bone!

(Grabs Lisette.)

LISETTE. *("Damsel in distress.")*

Help! Help!

CRISPIN/AMERICAN.

And by the way, I need a loan.

Ten thousand, or I burn this house to earth!

ERASTE.

You devil!

CRISPIN/AMERICAN.

HUNGH?!

ERASTE.

What hellhole gave you birth?

How dare you speak that way to Uncle? Vanish,

Beelzebub, and be forever banished

Not only from this house but from ...

CRISPIN.

(Your land?)

ERASTE.

                                        ... our land!

CRISPIN/AMERICAN.

Oh, please, sir, please, suspend yer wrathful hand!

I dint mean nothin' mean to ol' Geppetto!

See? Yer so tough I'm talkin' in falsetto!

ERASTE.

Now go! Or must I drive you out in Latin?

CRISPIN/AMERICAN.

No, sir. I'm gone. Get thee behind me, satin!

And damn the man who stops me or impedes me.

If anybody asks, *America needs me*!

(Crispin exits center.)

ERASTE.

Well, that should be the last of that grandee.

LISETTE.

Your sister must have mated with a tree —

And not the brightest gingko in her garden.

GERONTE.

That creature's not my nephew!

ERASTE and LISETTE.

                                        Beg your pardon?

GERONTE.

My sister was as fine as Belgian crepe.

How could she generate the Hairy Ape?

LISETTE.

He looked like you.

ERASTE.

                        The traits were undeniable.

GERONTE.

He wore a dog! He's certifiable!

LISETTE.

Another reason he deserves no boon!

Leave money to some transatlantic loon?

ERASTE.

Whose whole demeanor, sir, was one big F-you?

No, I cannot support my fellow nephew.

GERONTE.

Perhaps you're right. But if he was a fake ...

45

LISETTE.

All Yanks are like that, sir! For heaven's sake!

Ruffians who need to go to school again!

ERASTE.

They don't know wine or cheese.

LISETTE.

They're hooligans!

They'll cover this whole planet with their stench!

ERASTE.

Steal film from who invented it!

LISETTE and ERASTE.

The French!

ERASTE.

So he's a fake? It's esoterica!

GERONTE.

You're right! I disinherit all America!

I'll give his cash to someone not unruly.

To someone who deserves it!

ERASTE.

Me?

GERONTE.

Niece Julie!

I'm sure she could use double gold in scores.

ERASTE.

But, sir, if you'll excuse me, I've some chores ...

(Eraste exits center, quickly.)

LISETTE.

You did note how your nephew saved the day?

GERONTE.

Yes, and I'll compensate his brave display.

In view of prowess he evinced in plenty

I'm going to up his ten centimes to twenty.

The gall of that would-be acquisitor!

(Offstage knocking.)

What's this noise, now? Another visitor?

(Lisette exits center.)

Unless that's Lawyer Scruple, I don't want ...

(Crispin trips in as Julie, wearing an enormous padded dress and sausage curls. Lisette follows.)

CRISPIN/JULIE.
  Excuse me, sir. Are you Monsieur Geronte?
GERONTE.
  Good God!
CRISPIN/JULIE.
              Oh, Uncle, what a pleasure! Truly!
      What, you don't recognize me, sir? IT'S JULIE!
      COUNTESSE DE LA COCHON? CHÂTEAU DE SWINE?
GERONTE.
  You needn't shout at me. My hearing's fine.
CRISPIN/JULIE.
  Your other senses? Don't tell me they're failing!
(Waving, from six inches away.)
  I'm over here!
GERONTE.
              I *see* you.
CRISPIN/JULIE.
                      You're not ailing...?
GERONTE.
  This time of year a cold gets in my head.
CRISPIN/JULIE.
    That's queer! Some neighbors told me you were dead!
    How wonderful to find they were mistaken.
    But I forgot my gifts!
(Producing them from a capacious bag.)
                      A side of bacon ...
    A bag of pork rinds and some sausage twirls ...
    They're off the same hog as my sausage curls.
GERONTE.
  (Her note was sweet, but could this girl be gaucher?)
LISETTE.
  (I'll tell you this: She isn't strictly kosher.)
CRISPIN/JULIE.
    And as proof positive of who I am,
    Check out my portrait on this Polish ham.
    All for a man I honor like my mommy —
    Oh, and some cutlets and a small salami.
GERONTE.
  A kin at last who's kind and not a fool.
  A chair for her, Lisette.

CRISPIN/JULIE.
Oh, just a stool.
A mound will do. A tiny bump. A bevel.
I, sit with Uncle on a single level?
(Lisette brings "her" a stool.)
No, that's too tall.
LISETTE. *("Don't give me any crap, okay?")*
Yeah, well, it's *all we have.*
GERONTE.
My little niece, you are a healing salve.
(As "Julie" loudly bursts into tears.)
But why these tears?
("Julie" moans.)
This moan?
("Julie" sighs.)
That sigh so sweeping?
CRISPIN/JULIE.
You called me *little*, sir. That's why I'm weeping!
I was once brittle as a fishing pole
But victuals, kids, and pigs will take their toll —
For they with Life conspired like vicious plotters
To turn me to this mincing ham on trotters.
Just look at me, a sow in patchy twill,
So poor that I'm reduced to eating swill!
(A snorting sob into a hankie.)
Oh, oinkle, *Uncle*, then there was my marriage —
Dear Cyril, whom I'll let no man disparage!
Too bad the SOB kicked off so young.
He left me dirt-poor, and my boobs behung
With nine small infants, like some sucking necklace.
GERONTE.
You have nine children?
CRISPIN/JULIE.
Ten. So call me reckless.
Then when he's dead two years, to top our sins,
Out pops a complimentary set of twins!
GERONTE.
Twins? Two years after?
CRISPIN/JULIE.
Oh, Cyril was virile.

GERONTE.

But, Niece, what brings you to my door unbid?

CRISPIN/JULIE.

To see you, sir! My motives are unhid!

And to appall you with my tale of woe

So you in turn can leave me all your dough.

Your stocks, your bonds, what's hidden in your closet.

(Takes out a large piggy bank.)

See there? Miss Piggy's ready for deposit!

GERONTE.

I? Leave you all...?!

CRISPIN/JULIE.

                              Oh, sir, I pullulate,

I levitate, I ululate with thanks!

GERONTE.

But all I've left you's twenty thousand francs!

CRISPIN/JULIE.

You're joking. Twenty thousand? Why, it's piddling!

Anything less than everything's belittling.

You think I'd breed or suckle any brat

If I'd not get the goods your will begat?

Ah, well. I'll have to play my own rewarder —

By serving you with this restraining order.

(Shows a paper.)

GERONTE.

Restraining what?!

CRISPIN/JULIE.

                              It's inescapable.

You see, it says here you're incapable.

GERONTE.

Incapable? You crocodile! You dare?

CRISPIN/JULIE.

How else am I to get my proper share?

(Offstage knocking.)

GERONTE.

Goddamnit, what's that bloody noise out there?

(Isabelle enters, also as Julie, in a fat dress and sausage curls.)

ISABELLE/JULIE.

Excuse me!

GERONTE.
                    Help me, Jesus!
ISABELLE/JULIE.
                                    Uncle Jer?!
    You mean that you're not dead? You shock me cruelly!
    But what's the matter, sir? It's me! *(Oink, oink.)* It's Julie!
GERONTE.
    Yes, but ... Yes, but ...
ISABELLE/JULIE.
                            But what?
GERONTE.
                                    Is that you, too?
(Isabelle sees Crispin and screams.)
CRISPIN/JULIE.
    Who is this creature?
ISABELLE/JULIE.
                        What is *that*?
GERONTE.
                                    It's *you*!
CRISPIN/JULIE.
    Yes, I! The rightful heir to this man's plenty!
    I've twelve sick children. *(Oink.)*
ISABELLE/JULIE.
                            Really? I have twenty. *(Oink.)*
CRISPIN/JULIE.
    We live inside a barn. *(Oink.)*
ISABELLE/JULIE.
                            You have a roof? *(Oink.)*
CRISPIN/JULIE.
    We dine on husks.
ISABELLE/JULIE.
                        You opera-bouffe Tartuffe!
GERONTE.
    Enough, enough! But, Niece, you haven't brought
    Some nasty old restraining order...?
ISABELLE/JULIE.
                                    What?
    Of course not, Uncle! That thought's not arisen.
    No, I've a warrant ordering you to prison.
(Produces a paper.)

GERONTE.

    Prison?

ISABELLE/JULIE.

            Till I get all the gold I want.

    Why else bring Lady Piggy on this jaunt?

(Produces an even larger piggy bank.)

GERONTE.

    I don't know where I am.

(Eraste enters, also as Julie, in a fat dress and sausage curls, carrying a still-larger piggy bank.)

ERASTE/JULIE.

                  Uncle Geronte!

CRISPIN, GERONTE, ISABELLE, and LISETTE.

    Good God!

GERONTE.

           Oh, let me guess. You're Julie, too?

ERASTE/JULIE.

    Or Three. *(Oink.)*

GERONTE.

          I see you brought your trusty bank.

    Well *I* say you three piglets *all* are rank!

    Nor do I care which is my sibling's daughter.

    Remove your shanks and take your banks to slaughter!

    You'll not feed off my gold! I'm not your fork!

    I disbequeath you all! And swear off pork!

(Geronte exits right, followed by Lisette.)

CRISPIN/JULIE.

    Oh, sir, you treat me like this — me, a widow?

ISABELLE/JULIE.

    And me, a widow!

(Mountain echo, as he goes.)

ERASTE/JULIE.

            Ditto!

CRISPIN/JULIE.

                 Ditto…!

ISABELLE/JULIE.

                     Ditto…!

(Geronte is gone. Jubilation.)

ERASTE.

    Were we amazing?

ISABELLE.

We were brilliant, kiddo!

CRISPIN.

Well, those usurping relatives are finished!

ISABELLE.

We've still got work.

ERASTE.

My hopes are undiminished.

I snap my fingers in the face of dread.

Some angel's guiding me, with wings outspread!

(Lisette runs in.)

LISETTE.

Monsieur, monsieur...!

ERASTE.

He's on The Pot?

LISETTE.

He's dead.

CRISPIN, ERASTE, and ISABELLE.

He's *what?!*

LISETTE.

Stretched on the bed, completely still.

Sans breath, sans warmth, sans heartbeat ...

ISABELLE.

... and sans will.

ERASTE.

A temporary swoon, that's all it is.

LISETTE.

Monsieur, this isn't just a lack of fizz.

CRISPIN.

One of your magic laxatives can't spark him?

LISETTE.

The only question now is where to park him.

(They weep and wail, crying, "NO! NO!")

CRISPIN.

Hang on now, kids. Okay, we lost the fox.

But he left one thing in his hole.

ALL.

THE BOX!

ERASTE.

Lisette — the key!

LISETTE.

It's bonded to his leash!

ERASTE.

Well, see if it can reach here from his niche!

(Lisette runs out right.)

ISABELLE.

Eesh!

CRISPIN.

Eesh!

LISETTE.

I've got it!

(Lisette runs back in trailing the chain, but slams to a screaming halt just shy of The Box.)

No! We're short about one grommet!

ERASTE.

Then to the Mount we'll bring the dead Mohammed!

(Eraste and Crispin run out right.)

LISETTE. *(To us.)*

Okay, I grant you it's a bit macabre.

It's not the way we'd *like* things. It's a *job*!

(Eraste and Crispin reappear, carrying the limp Geronte.)

CRISPIN and ERASTE.

Corpse coming through!

ERASTE.

I'll get the key. You prop him.

(Eraste digs the key from Geronte's shirt and frees The Box while the others struggle to hold up the body.)

CRISPIN.

I've got him.

ISABELLE.

Someone brace his knees.

LISETTE.

Don't drop him!

ISABELLE.

We're losing him! We're losing him!

CRISPIN.

You stop him!

ISABELLE.

I have to sneeze. *ACHOO!*

GERONTE. *(Waking for a second.)*
                    Gesundheit!
ISABELLE.
                              Thanks.

    But wait! You're sure he's dead?
LISETTE.
                              As lumbered planks.

ERASTE.
    The Box has been unchained!
CRISPIN, ISABELLE, and LISETTE.
                    HURRAY!

ERASTE.
                              And in a jiff ...

    The Box has been unlocked!
CRISPIN, ISABELLE, and LISETTE.
                    HURRAY!

CRISPIN.
                    Let's lose the stiff.

ALL. *(Including Geronte.)*
                              HURRAY!
(Eraste and Crispin carry the body off. Lisette and Isabelle fall on their knees before The Box.)
ISABELLE and LISETTE.
    Almighty Box, for whom we have a yen,
    Please make us filthy, stinking rich. *Amen!*
(Eraste reenters.)
ERASTE.
    My friends, attend the blossoming of our scheme!
    One million francs!
ISABELLE.
                    Oh, darling, it's a dream!
(Eraste slowly opens The Box and looks inside.)
CRISPIN.
    Well, sir?
ERASTE. *(Producing a coin and a note.)*
                    One coin. One note. *"My First Centime."*
(They weep and wail, tearing their hair, crying, "NO! NO!")
CRISPIN.
    Stop! STOP! We know this million must be close.
    Let's be *more* motivated, not morose.

Lisette, sew tight your lips and watch the door.
Monsieur, we two will search beneath the floor
And frisk the place for any stray dinero.
Mam'selle, go home and be a chirping sparrow
Unto your mom, the radar dowager —
Who if she finds he's dead will be a howitzer.
(They join hands, Four Musketeers-like.)
Now all for one, and one ... The rest you know.
And here's to holy matri-money!

ALL.

Matri-money!

CRISPIN.

GO!

(They scatter as the clock whirs and makes its agitated farting noise. The curtain falls.)

End of Act One

ACT TWO

The same, a while later. Everyone is back in their own clothes.
As the curtain rises, Crispin is searching the room for money.

CRISPIN.

    Nothing in there ... Nope. Nope. Nothing behind ...
(Calls to next room.)

    You'd think we'd hit it, two of us combined ...
(Eraste enters from right, carrying wads of paper.)

    What's that?

ERASTE.

               The only treasure I could find.

CRISPIN.

    Don't look so miserable! At least you *got* some!

ERASTE.

    I had to wreck his potty for this flotsam.

    The total compensation for our caper?

    A measly forty thousand francs — in *paper*.

    Some IOUs, a ream of ancient stock ...
(The clock whirs, strikes one, and makes its agitated, farting chime.)

    If I had a pistol, I would cream that clock.

CRISPIN.

    And he's still in there, really — *you* know — dead?

ERASTE.

    He didn't grumble while I probed his bed.

    Three hours I've searched, expecting glittering eyefuls.

    What do we get? Some promissory trifles!
(Tosses the notes into The Box.)

CRISPIN.

    What trifles? We can float on forty K!

ERASTE.

    One drop of what a proper will would pay.

    What of the sea of money I expected?

    The ocean of centimes that he collected?

CRISPIN. *(Showing the centime they found in The Box.)*
His first memorial coin could come in handy.
ERASTE.
What for? To bribe my jailers? Buy some candy?
(Tosses the coin out the window.)
You know, this isn't avarice or greed.
I'll tell you what it is, Crispin ...
CRISPIN.
You mean the rise of the bourgeoisie and a proto-capitalist
society devoted to competition, consumerism, and cutthroat
self-promotion?
ERASTE.

       It's *need.*
That million would have let me marry! Breed!
I'm talking chromosomes! Man/woman! He/she!
CRISPIN.
Yeah, sure, the propagation of the specie.
Species, I mean.
ERASTE.
Alas, my friend! We're pigs in Fortune's poke,
Our fertile dreams gone up in sterile smoke!
CRISPIN.
You've just gone bonkers chasing after riches.
You think you're bad?
(Indicates the audience.)

       Check out *these* sonsabitches.
What can you do but hitch your pants and man up?
ERASTE.
But didn't you say you'd think some brilliant plan up?
How do we find my uncle's treasure hoard?
CRISPIN.
Hire a psychic? Fire up the Ouija board?
ERASTE.
Oh, thank you for that wisdom.
CRISPIN.

       Any time.
(Lisette enters from center.)
LISETTE.
Monsieur Eraste, the lawyer's here.

ERASTE.

                                      Sublime!

Each awful moment sires a fouler sibling.
So what's he doing?

LISETTE.

                           He's a lawyer: quibbling.

Should he come in left foot or right foot first?
And could he sue you if he trips?

ERASTE.

                                 I'm cursed!

LISETTE.

Oh, he's a tetchy one, thanks to his size.
A kaiser's ego in a pygmy's guise.

ERASTE.

Does he know Uncle's terminal condition?

LISETTE.

Not yet. But isn't it the law's tradition
Not to care, if he can send a bill?

ERASTE.

Not when a dead man *has to write a will!*
Not when his client's *morto-tissimus,*
Uploading boulders next to Sisyphus!
Crispin!

CRISPIN.

        Monsieur!

ERASTE.

                 Alas!

CRISPIN.

                     Alack!

ERASTE.

                         For woe!

CRISPIN.

How could a dead man write a ... write a ... *WHOA!!!*

LISETTE.

The juice is loose, monsieur! Crispin is thinking.

ERASTE.

How can you tell?

LISETTE.

                See that? That manic blinking?

CRISPIN. *(Thinking and blinking furiously.)*

Wait wait wait *wait*. It's crazy, but ... Why not...?

ERASTE.

Crispin, is it a plan?

CRISPIN.

Plan? It's a *plot*!

A vision sent by God!

ERASTE.

Of what?

CRISPIN.

Of clover —

And we're all in it! Wait! It's clouding over!

LISETTE.

Oh, damn this vision!

ERASTE.

Vision — please! Return!

Dream on, Crispin! Dream! Glow! Enkindle! Burn!

CRISPIN.

I got it! Yes! If I, if he ... That's clever ...

Then you, then me ... Not bad! But then ... However ...

LISETTE.

This lawyer isn't gonna wait forever.

(Crispin is still lost in complicated mental planning.)

Crispin! We got some bank-books to enhance!

CRISPIN.

Would you excuse me, babe? I'm in a trance.

(Goes back into it.)

So he says *blah*-blah ... I say cha-cha-*cha*,

He does the thing ... I do the tra-la-la ...

It's coming, kids, it's coming...! *YES! TA-DAA!*

My friends, I have outdone the algebra,

Out-thunk all thinkers Anglo, Frank, or Teuton,

Including Ike (that's what I call him) Newton.

LISETTE.

What is it?

CRISPIN.

An idea that's so ace

I bet you five you're gonna kiss my face.

Lisette, I need a set of Scrooge's clothes.

One of those sacks he wears, the bagged-out hose,

And don't forget the wig and fuzzy helmet,
That weird-ass front that hangs down like a pelmet,
For I shall be a hail-miser-well-met.
LISETTE.
But you don't mean...?!
CRISPIN.

Hey, darlin', shall we dance?

LISETTE. *(Grabbing Crispin's face and kissing it.)*
You living treasure! This was worth a trance!
(Lisette exits right.)
ERASTE.
You'll reunite my future and my lady's?
CRISPIN.
Boss, it's my *job* to pluck you outta Hades.
Get ready to be named sole legatee.
ERASTE.
Crispin, you are a genius!
CRISPIN.

C'est la vie.

ERASTE.
For this you shall be blessed for years in scores.
CRISPIN.
I've only one request.
ERASTE.

Name it. It's yours.

CRISPIN.
Don't let them hang me, sir! I'm just a pawn!
ERASTE.
Hang you? For what, Crispin?
CRISPIN.

Oh, sir. Come *AWN*.

The crime that you're about to perpetrate!
Of course, they'll hang you first ...
ERASTE.

Who, me?

CRISPIN.

Too late!

Here comes Lisette with all the needed trappings.
(Lisette reenters with a pile of Geronte's clothes.)

ERASTE.

They're going to *hang* me?

CRISPIN.

Sir, if you'd stop yapping

And lend a hand, our little show can start.

LISETTE.

One of his robes and caps.

CRISPIN.

Oh, very smart.

See there? I touch his stuff and it's seismotic!

I suddenly feel sclerotic, phlebotic,

Thrombotic, neurotic, and necrotic.

(With Lisette and Eraste's help, he dresses in Geronte's clothes.)

LISETTE.

As long as with the old man's seedy raiment

You're not infected by his dread of payment.

You will remember poor Lisette, now...?

CRISPIN. *(Geronte's voice.)*

Who?

Where are my fetid slippers? You, sir! You!

Fetch me a neckerchief and make it snappy!

(His own voice.)

These duds are magic. Geez, I'm feeling crappy!

My lungs are like a slough, my head's all snot.

And now this urge to merge with yonder pot ...

(Lisette pulls him back. He takes the cane and walks like Geronte.)

So what d'ya think, sir? Will I pass inspection?

ERASTE.

Oh, you've transcended that. It's resurrection!

The old man as he walked, or limped, in truth.

LISETTE.

You want to make some bread, set up a booth

And raise the dead for people for a living.

CRISPIN.

You powers of hell, whom men call unforgiving,

Send back a spirit from your haunted deep!

Restore to us Geronte, the king of cheap!

(He does thunder and lightning as Geronte stumbles in from right, looks around in a daze, and stumbles back out.)

Okay, I'm set. Lisette, bring on the shyster.
(Lisette exits center.)
Monsieur — the shutters. I may be a meister
Of transformation, but I need my light.
ERASTE. *(Closes the shutters.)*
Hermetically sealed up, all nice and tight.
Now pray to Venus that she's philanthropic.
CRISPIN.
I pray to Christ this lawyer is myopic!
(He sits in Geronte's chair. Lisette enters from center.)
LISETTE.
Your lawyer, sir.
CRISPIN/GERONTE.
                Send in the clown! He's late!
(Scruple enters from center. He is very short — the result of walking on his knees, which are cased in little shoes. He drags the train of a legal robe behind him.)
SCRUPLE.
Monsieur Geronte?
CRISPIN/GERONTE.
                Ah, there you are! But wait ...
Lisette, where is he?
SCRUPLE.
                Here, sir.
CRISPIN/GERONTE.
                Where's this lawyer?
SCRUPLE.
I'm here.
CRISPIN/GERONTE.
                What, did you leave him in the foyer?
Go search the house and find the SOB!
SCRUPLE.
Monsieur Geronte!
CRISPIN/GERONTE.
                I hear a voice.
SCRUPLE.
                        That's me!
CRISPIN/GERONTE.
Good God, what's that? Who're you? Speak up, you're far!

SCRUPLE.
I am Scruple — giant of the Paris bar!
CRISPIN/GERONTE.
A giant?
SCRUPLE.
To my clients and the courts,
A titan in the world of wills and torts!
You note this golden chain, my ruby ring?
Gotten by vetting *every tiny thing*?
I am a beagle, sir, being such a stickler
The legal board calls me "The Great French Tickler."
For, winkling out what's doubtful in a suit,
I eat minutiae!
CRISPIN/GERONTE.
Well, you're minute.
But have we met before? You know my mien?
SCRUPLE.
You don't recall you hired me sight-unseen?
CRISPIN/GERONTE.
You're *still* unseen!
SCRUPLE.
Of course, I know you faintly.
CRISPIN/GERONTE.
My greed? My oddball cap?
SCRUPLE.
To put it quaintly.
CRISPIN/GERONTE.
Well, as you know, I'm soon to reach our saintly ...
Hello?
SCRUPLE.
I'm here, monsieur.
CRISPIN/GERONTE.
... our saintly port.
And time being (like you, Titan) rather short,
I need a will, sir, tight and to the topic,
And *no small print*. Forget you're microscopic.
Write BIG!
SCRUPLE.
I'll make a note.

CRISPIN/GERONTE.

                    LARGE aspirations!

(Coughs.)

    You've read my memoir?

(Spits.)

                      Great Expectorations?

SCRUPLE.

    I don't believe …

CRISPIN/GERONTE.

               Be quiet. I've just one fret:

    That I'll kick off before this will is set.

    Who knows but fixing it in inky black

    Won't spark some freakish terminal attack?

(Has a wild "heart attack," slumps over "dead," then immediately rises.)

    Yes! Given the document we have in mind,

    I want to live to see this deed is signed.

SCRUPLE.

    On that account, sir, set your cares at rest.

    I know no man who's not survived the test

    Of setting down his ultimate desires.

(Crispin "dies" during:)

    It's not as if one's … bank of … mortal fires …

    Could be extinguished by the mere … *Monsieur?*

(Crispin wakes, only to start "dying" again.)

    … mere writing of a will. The act's a cure!

    Why, I've seen men who'd been the near-departed

    Rise up anew from their … *Monsieur!*

CRISPIN/GERONTE. *("Coming alive.")*

                      Who farted?

SCRUPLE.

    If you don't mind, I think we'd best get started.

(Noting Eraste and Lisette peering over his shoulder.)

    But lest we generate some legal cloud,

    No lookers-on, of course, can be allowed.

LISETTE.

    I can't leave him alone. This man's a baby!

CRISPIN/GERONTE.

    Gah-gah!

ERASTE.

          I'd happily leave, but Uncle, maybe …

CRISPIN/GERONTE.

These persons, sir, are so discreet, so sage,
They shred my every confidential page
By eating them like epicurean dishes.
SCRUPLE.

They eat your...?
CRISPIN/GERONTE.

Papers.
(Gives paper to Eraste and Lisette, who chew unhappily.)
SCRUPLE.

As the client wishes ...

Then let's begin. You are this will's testator? *["tes-TAY-tor"]*
CRISPIN/GERONTE.

How dare you, sir! I am a *what*?!
SCRUPLE.

Testator.

You hold the rights to vest what's vestable?
CRISPIN/GERONTE.

I am the holder of the testicle.
You're here to show how best one can invest it,
And keep my testicle from dying intestate!
SCRUPLE.

Yes, well, we start with standard boilerplate,
As, "I, Monsieur Geronte, do hereby state ... "
CRISPIN/GERONTE.

Hey! HEY! Did I not say let's hit the gas?
I'm dyin' up here!
SCRUPLE.

All right, we'll let that pass.
CRISPIN/GERONTE.

I'm passing some right now.
(Pauses to pass the gas.)

All right, I'm set.
SCRUPLE.

Now, are there any monies owed, or debt?
ERASTE.

Sir, given my uncle, we need hardly fret ...
CRISPIN/GERONTE

No, wait wait wait. I have some IOUs.
(Digs out some filthy, crumpled papers.)

From Gaston's Bar, two francs and forty sous ...
This one's for booze down at The Horny Goat,
Three francs and ten centimes ...

SCRUPLE.

I'll make a note.

Now to your obsequies? Your burial?

CRISPIN/GERONTE.

Oh, that. Just stick me in a carry-all.
Dump the cadaver in the nearest pit.
Nephew, you hear my wish?

ERASTE.

I'll see to it.

CRISPIN/GERONTE.

And nothing fancy, mind you. Nothing gaudy.
Forget the carry-all. Just toss my body
Into a cab and tell the driver, "*GO.*"
It'll be half a mile before he'll know.
To *stiff* a cabbie from beyond the grave!
To think of all the tips I could've saved
By riding dead! Ah, well. Too late to fix that.
But pay for funeral expenses? Nix that.
I wouldn't have it on my conscience ... *up there* ...
Anyone ran a tab on this affair.

SCRUPLE.

I'll make a note. Now, any legacies?

CRISPIN/GERONTE.

This part's a breeze. It is my ecstasy
And privilege to name sole testatee,
Leaving to him all goods, gold, property,
Deeds, ready money, furniture, rugs, plate,
All income payable to my estate,
My signet and the wiglet on my pate,
My dentures and what's hidden in my sock,
That ornamental chest, that ugly clock,
Also including, for nostalgia's sake,
That agitated farting noise it makes,
(Imitates the clock.)
While disinheriting all uncles, aunts,
Americans, cousins, nieces, potted plants,
As well as any bastards I've been blessed with

And several women I'd the joy to nest with,
In short all I possess, present or past,
I give my nephew (what's his name?) Eraste.
ERASTE.
O bitterness too bitter! Heavy cross!
O spite! That I must gain but by your loss!
SCRUPLE.
That's all?
CRISPIN/GERONTE.
Not quite.
ERASTE.
Not *quite?*
CRISPIN/GERONTE.
In recognition
Of five long years of good coition
(Correcting himself.)
nutrition,
I leave unto my faithful maid Lisette ...
LISETTE.
Oh, thank you, sir!
CRISPIN/GERONTE.
Girlfriend, don't thank me yet.
To her, whose tits are like some crystal *palais*, *["PAL-ay"]*
That she may wed Crispin, that faithful valet, *["VAL-ay"]*
And be insured against financial crash,
I leave her ...
ERASTE.
Yes?
CRISPIN/GERONTE.
A thousand francs in cash.
ERASTE.
What?!
CRISPIN/GERONTE.
Make that *new coins* in a handy tote.
You got that, Scrupulous?
SCRUPLE.
I'll make a note.
LISETTE.
Heaven bless you, master, with eternal light!

ERASTE.

So much for extra legacies.

CRISPIN/GERONTE.

Not quite.

I leave Crispin …

ERASTE.

Crispin? You've lost your mind!

CRISPIN/GERONTE.

Nephew, you've left your inside voice behind?

To *said Crispin* …

ERASTE.

Who causes only *grief!*

The man's a libertine, a brazen thief!

CRISPIN/GERONTE.

… a lad whose only flaw's being overzealous,

To him, despite the whinings of the jealous,

I leave a miniscule gratuity …

ERASTE.

Which is…?

CRISPIN/GERONTE.

Two thousand francs annuity.

ERASTE.

Two thou…? It's madness! It's fatuity!

CRISPIN/GERONTE.

Or would you rather that I made it three?

ERASTE.

No! *No!*

CRISPIN/GERONTE.

I *could* leave four, if three's too mingy.

Hell, make it *five!* I'm tired of being stingy!

What's more, without that clause this will is void!

Nephew, your thoughts?

ERASTE.

Oh, sir, I'm overjoyed.

CRISPIN/GERONTE.

Now have I any other pals who're needy…?

ERASTE.

(I'll kill you.)

CRISPIN/GERONTE.

… No. Why subsidize the greedy?

SCRUPLE.
   So is that all, monsieur?
CRISPIN/GERONTE.
                                    Yes, read that back.
ERASTE.
   (Not one more magnanimity attack.)
SCRUPLE.
   Now let me see here. "I, Monsieur," and so on.
   "One debt to Gaston's Bar ... "
(Geronte wanders in from right. He and Crispin are dressed exactly alike.)
ERASTE and LISETTE.
                    AAAAAAAAAAHHHH!
SCRUPLE.
                           What is it?
(Eraste and Lisette block Geronte before Scruple can see him.)
CRISPIN/GERONTE.
                                        Go on.
*(During the following, Geronte weaves about the stage as Eraste and
Lisette try to herd him back toward his room.)*
SCRUPLE.
   " ... to Gaston's Bar, two francs and forty sous ...
   The Horny Goat, et cetera, for some booze ...
   Testator's burial should run up no tab ...
   To be effected in a taxicab ... "
   I'll skip down to the major transferee.
   "I name my major (not sole) testatee
   Leaving to him all goods, gold, property,
   Deeds, ready money, furniture, rugs, plate,
   All income payable to my estate,
   My signet and the wiglet on my pate,
   My dentures and what's hidden in my sock,
   That ornamental chest, that ugly clock ... "
*(Geronte plops himself in his chair on Crispin's lap, hiding Crispin
from Scruple's view.)*
GERONTE.
   Where am I...?
SCRUPLE.
                       Beg your pardon, sir?
GERONTE.
                                            Where am I?

SCRUPLE.

You're in your sitting room. Remember?

CRISPIN/GERONTE. *(Working Geronte's arms like a puppet.)*

Damn! I

Forgot! Read on, read on.

SCRUPLE.

"... that ugly clock,

Including ... "

GERONTE.

Who are you?

(Scruple looks up. Geronte and Crispin are still.)

SCRUPLE.

"... that ugly clock,

Including also for nostalgia's sake,

That agitated farting noise it makes ... "

(Imitates the clock.)

GERONTE.

Who are you?

SCRUPLE.

Sir, I am your lawyer, Scruple!

The fleck there at the center of your pupil?

Oh, you can't see me? I'll approach the chair ...

CRISPIN/GERONTE. *(Waving him back with Geronte's hand.)*

No, stay right where you are.

SCRUPLE.

Now, I was where...?

GERONTE.

Who are you?

SCRUPLE.

Damn it, sir, I've had my fill!

CRISPIN/GERONTE.

You keep this up, how can I make my will?

(Madame Argante enters from center, followed by Isabelle.)

MADAME ARGANTE.

Monsieur Eraste! What is this? What's going on here?

I know that something's up. My daughter's *cheer*

Is so nonstop it must be artificial.

I sniff a plot — some sneaky interstitial

Attempt to pull whole sheep over my eyes!

Hello, Monsieur Geronte.

(Crispin waves Geronte's hand. Seeing Geronte alive, Isabelle screams. To Eraste.)

You won't disguise
This ruse, and somehow I've a deep suspicion
Your uncle's health's the news — that his condition
Is terminal and you've concealed that fact.

GERONTE.

Who're you?

MADAME ARGANTE.

You see? His brain's gone non-intact!

GERONTE.

Who're you?

MADAME ARGANTE.

Monsieur Geronte, it's Eulalie!

GERONTE.

Who're you?

MADAME ARGANTE.

It's EULALIE!

CRISPIN/GERONTE.

Eulalie? Trulily…?

MADAME ARGANTE.

Trulily!

(To Eraste.)

He's ready for his funeral eulogy!

(Unnoticed by her, Geronte gets up and wanders the room again.)

SCRUPLE. *(Seeing two Gerontes.)*

Good God!

MADAME ARGANTE.

What's that?

SCRUPLE.

I think I'm seeing duple!

MADAME ARGANTE. *(Indicating Scruple.)*

What is that creature?

ERASTE.

That's the lawyer, Scruple.

SCRUPLE.

The Greek colossus of the Paris bar!

MADAME ARGANTE.

You're an *iota*, sir, that's what you are!

(To Eraste.)

You let him lapse into this senseless haze.
Well, I will sue your *ass*, to mint a phrase.
ERASTE.
But what you see's the existential daze
That comes of having written up one's will!
MADAME ARGANTE.
You mean — it's made?
ERASTE.

                             That's why he seems so ill!
Exhausted from the act of mere bequeathing,
From facing his mortality, he's seething
With questions all of us in time must face.
GERONTE.
Where am I?
ERASTE.

               Who am I? What is my place
In this mad universe *which I must EXIT*?
Exit, I say, must exit, *exit, EXIT*!
(Geronte staggers out right. Lisette follows him.)
ERASTE.
As for this will, you wouldn't want to hex it ...
MADAME ARGANTE.
You're hopeful? And your hopes are testable?
ERASTE.
Madame, I am my uncle's testicle!
Or, if not testicle, say, golden cup.
Is that not true, monsieur?
SCRUPLE.

                   Well, not ...

ERASTE.

                     Shut. Up!
And just to show I beat the long phalanx,
Consider this:
(Opens The Box.)

             some forty thousand francs!
In paper, but a rich engagement gift.
MADAME ARGANTE.
My boy, please pardon me if I seemed miffed
Or chastened you beneath your future roof.
He's left you *all*, you say...?

ERASTE.
                                        Is this not proof?
MADAME ARGANTE.
    I know it's merely scrip and paper stocks
    But may I ... for a moment ... grip ... *The Box?*
(Eraste puts it in her arms. We briefly hear an angelic choir.)
    I feel as if I've peered beyond the veil!
    But if this all turns out to be some tale ...
CRISPIN/GERONTE.
    Madame, I vow you'll not be disappointed.
    Eraste's my sole (well, almost sole) anointed.
MADAME ARGANTE.
    "Al*most*"...? He's not the only legatee?
CRISPIN/GERONTE.
    Small gifts to servants to remember me ...
MADAME ARGANTE.
    To *servants?*
CRISPIN/GERONTE.
                        Plus, what I've bequeathed to *you* ...
MADAME ARGANTE.
    You left something ... to *me?*
CRISPIN/GERONTE.
                                        Yes, you! The glue
    Unto my greed, the paste of my tight fist!
SCRUPLE.
    You left her what? Monsieur, I must insist —
CRISPIN/GERONTE.
    That as to what it is we all stay dumb?
    (The woman's mad!) That we conceal the sum?
MADAME ARGANTE.
    Don't tell me. No, just let me dream and want!
    That you should leave me something...? You, Geronte!
    You who know stocks and bonds and how to pick 'em!
    You who are stuck to gold as if with Stickum!
    That you, who'd only part from it with shears,
    Give *me* a piece of what to you adheres...?
    O, sir, I am not worthy of this debt!
    The figure is irrelev ... What'd I get?
ERASTE.
    The will is sealed.

MADAME ARGANTE.
                              No matter. I divine it.
SCRUPLE.

One small formality. Monsieur must sign it.
(Lisette enters from right.)
LISETTE.

Excuse me, sir, but I've just had a tweet.

He's dead at last.
MADAME ARGANTE.
                              Who's dead?
ERASTE.
                                        Her parakeet.
MADAME ARGANTE.

Stuff the damn bird! Bring me a quill and ink!
(Lisette gets them.)
CRISPIN/GERONTE.

I don't know why, I feel about to sink ...
MADAME ARGANTE.

You'll not die now! Take this and sign that, mister!
CRISPIN/GERONTE.

I can't! I'm weak! I'm limp! I have this blister!
MADAME ARGANTE.

What would compel your hand to get this signed?
CRISPIN/GERONTE.

The Kama Sutra somehow comes to mind.

But, *would* you grant a dying man a favor —

A final sign of friendship I might savor?
MADAME ARGANTE.

I'll do it, yes! Whatever size or flavor

If it will help you sign and keep me CALM!
CRISPIN/GERONTE.

Good. Rub your head and belly with your palm.
MADAME ARGANTE.

I beg your pardon, sir?!
CRISPIN/GERONTE.
                              Ah, what a balm

It were unto a sickly man to view that!

You know? Like this...?
(Demonstrates.)

MADAME ARGANTE.
                              No, I will not do *that*!
CRISPIN/GERONTE. *(Laying down the quill.)*
    Well, I won't beg …
MADAME ARGANTE. *(Rubbing belly, patting head.)*
                              How's this?
CRISPIN/GERONTE.
                              Oh, yes, that's good!
    Waggle your tongue!
(Madame Argante goes "La la la la la.")
                              Now maybe if you stood
    On just one leg! Now Scruple! Everybody!
    And counterclockwise! Eulalie, you're muddy!
    All right, I'll sign!
(All stop and gather around as he signs the paper very slowly.)
                              "G … E … R … " Guide my hand.
MADAME ARGANTE. *(Moving his hand for him very quickly.)*
    " … O … N … T … E."
SCRUPLE.
                              The witnesses.
(Eraste and Lisette sign in record time.)
MADAME ARGANTE.
                              The sand.
(Dumps sand all over the signatures.)
CRISPIN/GERONTE.
    Wow, that was fun! And look at you, all sweaty.
    I swear to God, I'm semi-cured already!
ERASTE.
    Lisette, you want to tend your little pet?
SCRUPLE.
    I'm not a PET!
ERASTE.
                              Her parakeet.
LISETTE.
                              You bet.
(Lisette exits.)
SCRUPLE.
    May I please go?
ERASTE.
                              Bra*vo*, monsieur! Well done!

75

SCRUPLE.

As chaos, yes, perhaps this was well-run.
A travesty in every other wise.
Humiliated but aerobicized,
I'll take my leave now if you've no objection
And bring a copy back for your inspection —
That is to say, *if you can make me out.*
Should you have codicils — please! Take me out
And drill me with a pistol shot or two,
Then hail my corpse a cab to Kathmandu! Adieu!
(Scruple exits center.)

MADAME ARGANTE.

Though miniature, he casts a major damper.
Well, Isabelle and I must also scamper.
Oh, please don't worry for this little box.
I'll put it somewhere safe and oil the locks.
You have no need for it, there's nothing pressing.
(Crispin signals, "Don't let her take The Box!" Madame Argante notices the gestures and Crispin turns them into a sign of the cross.)

ERASTE.

But look, my uncle's giving us his blessing.

MADAME ARGANTE.

Monsieur, you've made a worthy couple rich!

CRISPIN/GERONTE.

My dear, you are an avaricious bitch!

MADAME ARGANTE.

Thank you.

CRISPIN/GERONTE.

I've but one wish I wish were gratified:
A tiny parting peck from nephew's bride...?

ISABELLE.

With all my heart.

CRISPIN/GERONTE.

Where are you...?
(Crispin grabs Isabelle and gives her a good one.)

ERASTE.

All right, fella!

CRISPIN/GERONTE.

I can die happy now!

MADAME ARGANTE.

                              Come, Isabella.
(Madame Argante exits center.)
ISABELLE.

    I couldn't stop her, she was on a tear.
ERASTE.

    Well, let her rip. Come grip your millionaire.
ISABELLE.

    Ah, mon amour!
ERASTE.

                    Je t'aime!
ISABELLE.

                              Tu m'aimes?
ERASTE.

                                        De tout mon coeur!

    Tu pars?
ISABELLE.

              Je dois!
ERASTE.

                        Au 'voir!
ISABELLE.

                              À tout à l'heure!
(Isabelle exits center.)
CRISPIN.

    Well, I don't care what anybody says.
    I am a one-man Comédie Française!
(Getting out of Geronte's clothes.)
    This wig did me so well, I'm sad to doff it.
ERASTE.

    Who knew that you would don it to such profit?
    What were you thinking? An *annuity*?
    Five thousand francs?
CRISPIN.

                    A superfluity.
ERASTE.

    A thousand to Lisette?
CRISPIN.

                        It's chicken feed!
ERASTE.

    Grade-A organic!

CRISPIN.
                    Well, my chick's in need.
ERASTE.
    And so will *I* be, bankrolling your squeezes.
CRISPIN.
    It's *love*. It's *charity*. Take some tips from Jesus.
    But hey, this will is not to your desire?
    We'll call him back and toss it on the fire!
    Lisette! Get Scruple!
ERASTE.
                    No!

CRISPIN.
                    You're satisfied?

    Lisette!
ERASTE.
            No, wait!
CRISPIN.
                    You're good?

ERASTE.
                            I'm *gratified*.
(Lisette enters from right, obviously upset.)
LISETTE.
    Monsieur...!
CRISPIN.
                    You know, though, this near-death experience,
    Which was right up there with your best Shakespeareans ...
LISETTE.
    Crispin...!
CRISPIN.
                    It's put me in a pensive mood.
    (One sec.) It's fed my tendency to brood.
    You know — the tears in things, life's evanescence.
LISETTE.
    Monsieur...!
CRISPIN.
                    What are we? One brief day's fluorescence!
    Just look at Uncle G. Alive at dawn
    (One moment, hon) and now he's "G" for *gone*.
    This poor old man whom nothing can revive ...

LISETTE.

    Crispin ...

CRISPIN.

                  What is it, darling?

LISETTE.

                                         He's alive!

CRISPIN and ERASTE.

    GHHAAAAAAAAHHHHHHHH!

LISETTE.

    I go in there, he's ice-cold on the bedding.

    Next thing I know — he's dressing for his wedding!

    His Sunday shirt and shoes, a coat to match.

CRISPIN.

    Oh, *jeez*! You mean we gotta start from *scratch*?

ERASTE.

    Remember those gendarmes arresting you?

CRISPIN.

    Hey, I was kidding! I was *testing* you.

ERASTE.

    We'll visit you in jail. We'll bring you food.

CRISPIN.

    You'll visit *me...*?

ERASTE.

                       That tendency to brood

    Might help you when you're climbing up the scaffold.

CRISPIN.

    You mean this was some kinda *crime*? I'm baffled!

LISETTE.

    Monsieur Eraste, you know you're in this, too.

    And now our standard question ...

CRISPIN, ERASTE, and LISETTE.

                          What to do.

CRISPIN.

    O Fate! O Fortune! Fie this effing fettle!

ERASTE.

    Lisette is right. We have to show our mettle.

    I'll show you mine.

LISETTE.

                    And mine.

ERASTE.

Crispin? Be bold!

CRISPIN.

Okay. I only hope our mettle's gold.

GERONTE. *(Offstage.)*

Eraste?!

LISETTE. *(To Eraste, who's leaving.)*

What are you doing?

ERASTE.

Saving my skin!

(Eraste exits center.)

CRISPIN.

Well, that was fast. My master's mettle's tin.

(Geronte enters in a dandy outfit, all spruced up.)

GERONTE.

Good morning, all! Or is it afternoon?
One-thirty, is it! Lord, was that a swoon!
Like getting sucked into a dirty funnel!
But wait ... Now I recall a long, dark tunnel
Opened before me! At its end bright lights —
And Grandma*ma*, in very strange white tights ...
At which I woke and thought, *Lord*, what a dummy!
I'm rich as God, yet live here like a mummy!
For what, this urge to scrimp and hoard and save?
It's not as if I'll splurge when in my grave.
But what's the news? Don't let my chatter bar you.

LISETTE.

One question, sir.

GERONTE.

Yes, ask away.

LISETTE.

Who *are* you?

GERONTE.

A man reborn to this world's lofty scene,
Inhaling life's proverbial coffee bean.
But wait a moment ... Why're the shutters closed?

CRISPIN.

What shutters? Those?

GERONTE. *(Sees Crispin's costume, left lying.)*
                    I don't recall these clothes ...
LISETTE.
     What clothes? Oh, *those?*
GERONTE.
                                        That was the implication.
     Perhaps you could provide an explication
     Of everything that passed here during my swoon?
LISETTE.
     Pure pandemonium, sir. The house bestrewn,
     Just as you see, the moment it befell you.
     You'd not believe the ... Well, Crispin can tell you.
CRISPIN.
     Who, me? Oh, sir, you'd not believe the scene.
     Me, madly shutting shutters shut, to screen
     Your rolling eyes. You, tearing off your clothing
     While shouting "Lies! Lies! Lies!" as if in loathing
     Of your old odious personality.
     "Burn these!" you cried. "They're greed, they're malady!"
     (A very handsome suit there, by the way.)
     Your nephew doing CPR, to stay
     The hand of death and lengthen out your days.
     Lisette here, plotzing ... You would be ...
GERONTE.
                                                        Amazed?
CRISPIN.
     Amazed.
GERONTE.
          Where *is* Eraste...?
LISETTE.
                                        Ah, sir, you're going to shiver.
     Thinking you dead, he threw himself ...
GERONTE.
                                                  The *river?*
LISETTE.
     The foyer. Totally inconsolable.
     The grief? The weeping?
CRISPIN.
                         Uncontrollable.

GERONTE.
Well, bring him in. I long to see the boy,
If nothing else so he can share the joy
Of seeing me wed to ...
LISETTE.

Isabelle.

GERONTE.

Christina...?

Serena...?
LISETTE.
ISABELLE!
GERONTE.

Thank you. *Georgina.*

CRISPIN.
I'll lead my master, sir, to the arena —
Half-dead himself, no doubt, from sheer despair.
If not half-bald from tearing out his hair.
(Crispin exits center.)
GERONTE.
But this reminds me. My estate! My heir!
Did Scruple come?
LISETTE.

No. Yes.

GERONTE.

"No? Yes?" Which is it?

(Offstage knocking.)
LISETTE.
See that? His punctuality's exquisite,
For there's the little bastard now.
GERONTE.

Well? Run!

(Lisette turns to leave as Crispin enters, leading a reluctant Eraste.)
LISETTE. *(Aside to Crispin as she goes.)*
I'll stall the lawyer. You stall Number One.
(Lisette exits.)
CRISPIN.
Come, master, come. Behold this boon we've won.
ERASTE.
Alas, what bliss, what happiness unbounded.
How mis ... How wonderful to find our fears unfounded.

82

GERONTE.

Dear boy, these transports come as no surprise.
I know your bent to sentimentalize.
But you were right!

ERASTE.

                              I was?

GERONTE.

                                        To play my proctor.
To hell with price, I'm going to find a doctor!
I'll live to ninety if I mind my health!

ERASTE.

Well, death could always visit you by stealth …

(He is about to strangle Geronte. Crispin restrains him. Lisette reenters during the following)

GERONTE.

But listen, why dwell on mortality?
I'm tubing toward connubiality!
In light of which — ah, there you are, Lisette —
I'm going to guarantee you *get yours yet*.
Leave you some few centimes? What was I thinking!
I have some forty thousand francs, not clinking
But safe in paper, hidden in my commode.
A sort of "privy purse."
Lisette, where are you slinking? Find that lode.
They're for Eraste, in honor of my nuptial!
What's wrong? You look aghast.

ERASTE.

                                        Oh, sir, my cup shall
O'erflow with … something at your wedding vows.
But that's reward enough, seeing you espoused.
What use have I for forty thousand francs?

GERONTE.

To live life well! So please — no specious thanks.
Bring them, Lisette.

(Lisette goes into slo-mo.)

                              Arriba, la paloma!

LISETTE.

Monsieur, I think it's my turn for a coma.

GERONTE.

Shall I go? Fine. Then so I will — with speed.

ERASTE.

No, Uncle — Uncle, really, there's no need.
I swear, sir, I don't need them ... overly.

GERONTE.

Are you three putting something over me?

LISETTE.

Over you?

CRISPIN.

Over *you*?

ERASTE.

Who, Uncle? *Us?*

(Scruple enters from center.)

SCRUPLE.

Monsieur Geronte?

GERONTE.

Who's *this* homunculus?

Oh, Scruple, is it? For our rendezvous?

SCRUPLE.

Yes, I am Scruple, sir, but ... who are *you?*

GERONTE.

I am Geronte.

SCRUPLE.

Oh, please. These eyes can see.
May I request some personal ID?

GERONTE.

It's true we've never met.

SCRUPLE.

Not met?

GERONTE.

Not yet.

SCRUPLE.

Whom did I meet?

GERONTE.

Meet when?

SCRUPLE.

My previous jaunt.

GERONTE.

Your previous...? Sir, I tell you, I'm Geronte!

SCRUPLE.

Somewhat transfigured.

GERONTE.

So? I *am* your client!

SCRUPLE.

I marvel that reality's that pliant.

GERONTE.

I marvel at how long you've kept me waiting.

SCRUPLE.

Some half an hour?

GERONTE.

Some half a *day*, debating
Whether I'd ever find you in my sight.

SCRUPLE.

If that's another crack about my height,
I'll leave right now! *"Hello? Hello? Where ARE you?"*

GERONTE.

You're so bizarre I'm shocked they don't disbar you.
I hope you've cleared your offices of snakes.

SCRUPLE.

Snakes?

GERONTE.

Pythons! Cobras! *Fangs*, for heaven's sake,
Damning to Tennessee young healthy men!

SCRUPLE.

Tennessee?

ERASTE.

Tennessee!

SCRUPLE.

Well, here we go — again.

GERONTE.

Again's a bit obscure, but I'll ignore it.
Besides, I want no conflict. I deplore it
Still more today when all that's cruel or snide
Subsides before the joy of groom and bride —
A girl whose beauty every ill acquits.

SCRUPLE. *(Indicating Lisette.)*

You mean this woman and her crystal tits?

GERONTE.

No, I mean *me*! That is, my wife-to-be.

SCRUPLE.

You didn't mention any wife to *me*.

GERONTE.
I didn't mention when?
SCRUPLE.
                          This hour just past!
GERONTE.
Sir, your obscurity leaves me aghast.
No matter. Business calls, so grab a quill.
You know the task at hand. I need a will.
SCRUPLE.
You need...?
GERONTE.
                  A will.
SCRUPLE. *(Producing a document.)*
                          This will...?
GERONTE.
                  Good Lord, you're sloppy!
My *own* will, sir, not someone else's copy!
SCRUPLE.
This *is* your will.
GERONTE.
                          I *have* no will, you wen!
How could I?
SCRUPLE.
So, you want ... a *new* will, then...?
GERONTE.
Fine! Call it new! I've just one major fret.
SCRUPLE.
That you could die before the will is set?
GERONTE.
How did you know?
SCRUPLE.
                          You *said* it, FIE ON *ME*!
Now what're you gonna do? Go DIE ON ME?
(Imitates Crispin's wild heart attack.)
·   Would that be your response? Your fun retort?
GERONTE.
The price one pays for hiring someone short!
But wait. Are lookers-on like these allowed?
Might they not generate some legal cloud?

SCRUPLE.

But aren't these persons so discreet and sage
They shred your every confidential page
By gobbling them as snacks? Or were they faking?

GERONTE.

What medication, sir, have you been taking?
They *eat* my documents? Pray tell, what for?

SCRUPLE.

A question I'd've asked in days of yore —
When I was sane. Before these brain attacks
Made me see two of you on double tracks.

GERONTE.

I will ignore your mad hallucination
To finish this before my inhumation.
My debts no doubt come first. Well? Is it true?

SCRUPLE.

Monsieur, you are a course in déjà vu.
For I foresee your words as from afar.
Debt obligations? Sure!

(Takes out bills.)

There's Gaston's Bar...

GERONTE.

There's *what*?!

SCRUPLE.

Your bills for booze.

GERONTE.

My bills for WHAT?
Where did you get these things?

SCRUPLE.

From YOU, you BUTT!

What of your burial in a city cab?
Oh, you've decided you don't want that? FAB!
You note I'm crossing out IN BOLD? *Small hint.*
For God forbid there be the least *small print*!

GERONTE.

What is that, what's that document you're scratching?

SCRUPLE.

The testament you spent this morning hatching!

GERONTE.

I wrote my will?

SCRUPLE.
>You did.

GERONTE.
>Today?

SCRUPLE.
>Of course!

Apparently you've since had buyer's remorse!

GERONTE.

Eraste, you saw me write this?

ERASTE.
>What?

GERONTE.
>This deed?

You're down here as a witness to the screed.

ERASTE.

I have no legal training on this head.

I pass, and let Crispin speak in my stead.

GERONTE.

You saw me write this?

CRISPIN.
>You mean, did I "see" you?

Well, not exactly. Some man who could *be* you ...

Vaguely ... was here in something like that chair.

A sort of *aura*, far as I'm aware.

SCRUPLE.

That *he* says he was here, well, that's the jackpot!

I've *never met this man*!

CRISPIN.
>This, from a crackpot

Who said we scarf your papers with a spoon?

Plus don't forget, sir, don't forget *your swoon*.

GERONTE.

It's true, I had a transient caesura ...

LISETTE.

Monsieur, your seizure was bravura!

You *do* remember sending for this loon...?

GERONTE.

I do.

LISETTE.
>This deed?

GERONTE.

       I don't.

LISETTE.

          Well, there's your swoon!

CRISPIN.

 And you remember your Kentucky cousin?

 And Lady Pig, who littered by the dozen?

GERONTE.

 I do.

CRISPIN.

     And leaving me some trifling boon?

GERONTE.

 I don't.

CRISPIN.

      Your mind got stifled by the swoon!

GERONTE.

 How odd. I must have been completely blotto!

ERASTE.

 And that explains this lawyer's obbligato!

 Apparently you wrote this thing, you see?

 Behold your signature. Fait accompli!

CRISPIN.

 It's good enough for me.

LISETTE.

       And me.

CRISPIN.

         'Nuff said.

(Madame Argante and Isabelle enter from center. Madame Argante is carrying The Box.)

MADAME ARGANTE.

 I just now heard the news. So is he dead?

GERONTE.

 Not yet.

(Seeing him alive, Madame Argante and Isabelle scream.)

     Do I seem pounding on death's door?

MADAME ARGANTE.

 But one aquainted with the facts here swore

 She saw you stretched as if in effigy.

GERONTE.

 It was a momentary lethargy,

A swoon from whose effects I'm reeling still.
It seems while thus cocooned I wrote my will.
MADAME ARGANTE.
   You did.
GERONTE.
        I did?
MADAME ARGANTE.
             Sir, am I not your glue?
Your trusty mucilage to all that's true?
Of course you wrote it, and it's so well-written!
GERONTE.
   I left it all to Kitten?
SCRUPLE.
             STOP! What kitten?
GERONTE.
   Georgina here, the miss with whom I'm smitten.
My lawyer, Scruple.
MADAME ARGANTE.
           We met, previously.
I hope you'll pardon devious old me,
But you said "smitten" in that tangled thread.
Does that portend you still intend to wed?
GERONTE.
   Of course I do! I wonder you should ask it.
But don't you want to check that clumsy casket?
MADAME ARGANTE.
   If you don't mind, I'd rather cuddle it, please.
GERONTE.
   I've one just like it.
MADAME ARGANTE. *(Darkly, to Eraste.)*
          Really? *Quelle surprise.*
GERONTE.
   Well, since this will is made I may as well hear it.
ISABELLE.
   And God forbid there be some snag to queer it.
   (Are we about to die?)
ERASTE.
          (Or something near it.)
GERONTE.
   Well, Scruple?

SCRUPLE.

        No! I disavow this deed!

For I suspect there's something fishy...!

GERONTE.

                        Read!

SCRUPLE.

It's not just fishy, sir — it's *WHALE-SIZE* fishes!

Fine. You see nothing shady, or suspicious.

To "hit the gas" we'll skip name, place, and date ...

ISABELLE.

Oh, no, please read it! I love boilerplate!

I gorge on formulaic legal prose.

Who else?

CRISPIN.

      Me!

LISETTE.

         Me!

ERASTE.

           Me!

ISABELLE.

              Me! Since none oppose ...

CRISPIN, ERASTE, and ISABELLE.

Boilerplate! Boilerplate!

GERONTE.

Let's get this done before my final rest.

Forego the filler. What's my first bequest?

SCRUPLE.

"In recognition of five years' coition ... "

GERONTE.

Coition?!

SCRUPLE.

      Pardon me. "Of *good* coition."

Pardon me. Wrong again! "Of good *nutrition*,

I leave Lisette a thousand francs in cash."

GERONTE.

I *what*?!

LISETTE.

      Sir, I am speechless, I'm abashed!

I never dreamed with my bad attitude

You'd ever show such lavish gratitude.

91

GERONTE.
A thousand francs?!
SCRUPLE.
"Delivered in a tote … "
GERONTE.
A *tote*?!
SCRUPLE.
No tote?
GERONTE.
No tote.
SCRUPLE.
I'll make a note.
CRISPIN.
Monsieur, it may seem incongruity.
You left me, too, a small gratuity.
GERONTE.
How much?
CRISPIN.
Five thousand francs annuity.
GERONTE.
Five *THOUSAND*?
CRISPIN.
See? I also was amazed.
But hey — what can you get for that these days?
GERONTE.
I am amazed I missed this spectacle.
SCRUPLE.
You want to hear about your testicle?
GERONTE.
NO!
SCRUPLE.
You endowed it with a legacy …
GERONTE.
Fine. Read me that.
SCRUPLE.
"It is my ecstasy
To designate as major legatee,
Leaving to him all goods, gold, property … "
GERONTE.
Skip that!

SCRUPLE.

                    Et cetera ... "Hidden in my sock,
My ornamental chest, that ugly clock."
(Imitates the clock.)
GERONTE.
    Enough!
SCRUPLE.

                It's there, you see? Straight off my plume.
GERONTE.
    Just tell me, pray: I leave this all to whom?
SCRUPLE.
    "My nephew, what's his name, Eraste."
ISABELLE.

                                That swoon ...

GERONTE.
    Enough of swoons!
CRISPIN.

                    Or maybe you were plastered.
SCRUPLE.
    And then you disinherited your bastards.
GERONTE.
    My what? So I have bastards in the bargain?
ERASTE.
    That word, sir? "Bastards"? That's just legal jargon.
SCRUPLE.
    Then we all rubbed our heads and wagged our tongues.
(They all show how, going "La la la la la.")
GERONTE.
    Has my whole frontal cortex come unslung?!
SCRUPLE.
    "Signed by Geronte, as witnessed by ... " and so on.
CRISPIN.
    Well done, sir! *This* is why you've got that glow on.
    Because you've done good deeds for those you love.
GERONTE.
    You plotted this with them. You're hand-in-glove.
SCRUPLE.
    I write what's said! I'm an amanuensis!
GERONTE.
    But why would I, unless I'd left my senses,

Bequeath a bounty to a scamp like this,
A pile to her, or in parenthesis,
Leave everything to him from bonds to bedding
Intended for this woman whom I'm wedding?
Why leave to lunatics whole grand estates
For rubbing abdomens and patting pates?

MADAME ARGANTE.

Pardon, sir. No. Your senses weren't bereft.
This was conspiracy! Extortion! Theft!
For while you languished, void of any motion —
Knocked out, no doubt, but some rare Chinese potion
Or hypnotized by thugs from Samarkand —
No matter. They, monsieur, they forced your hand!

GERONTE.

By thugs from Samarkand?!

MADAME ARGANTE.

       It was a *crime*.
I marvel that your nephew's marked with grime,
But Izzy here's on fire to say "I do."

GERONTE.

Thank God, at least there's one of you who's true.

ISABELLE.

Good sir, I too deserve your righteous thunder,
For I was also party to this plunder.

GERONTE.

You'd decimate me with so cruel a taunt?
Those forty thousand francs — that's what I want!

ERASTE.

They're gone, sir.

GERONTE.

    Gone? Gone where?

CRISPIN, ERASTE, ISABELLE, and LISETTE.

         Madame Argante!

GERONTE.

Am I in France, or pirate-strewn Siam?
Is there *no one* who's innocent?

SCRUPLE.

       I am.

ERASTE.

Sir, didn't you just now claim you'd needs be mad

To give away so blindly all you had?
Well, I maintain you hadn't lost your senses —
You'd found them. In your swoon, without defenses,
You showed your *true* self: liberal, generous, kind.
You had regained, not lost, your natural mind.
GERONTE.
To leave one sou to you were gross miscarriage.
ERASTE.
Well then my true loss isn't gold, it's marriage.
GERONTE.
Marriage? To whom?
ERASTE.

              Georgina. *Isabelle.*
Whose infinite appeal, sir, you know well
From having been yourself her beauty's victim.
Who, just by being, turns love into a dictum.
GERONTE.
So you mean *marriage* sparked this mad display?
ERASTE and ISABELLE.
It did.
CRISPIN and LISETTE.

      Us, too.
GERONTE.

              Why didn't you all just *say*?
Confer with me, inform me, make me wiser?
CRISPIN.
Because you were a rotten, stinking miser!
As blind as money! Deaf as any ox!
(Impersonating Geronte, as before.)
   Lisette, my gold! Invigorate The Box!
   What's that, sir? Help the world? Improve man's lot?
   You want me, I'll be curled up on The Pot!
SCRUPLE.
Ah-HA! My well-known insight leaps the gap:
You were that man (or someone) *in a cap*!
The elephant in here at last comes clean!
GERONTE.
That elephant's irrelevant!
(To Crispin.)

             You mean ...

That's what I was? So keenly cold? So tart?
Mine eyes are opened through this servant's art!
And let me toss this thought into the cup:
If people hope you dead, you have *fucked up*.
So now as Lazarus twice or thrice reborn
Let me spill you your due from Plenty's horn!
CRISPIN.
You mean I'll get that small annuity?
GERONTE.
As payment for your ingenuity.
LISETTE.
I get my thou, to check in at the Ritz?
GERONTE.
Two thou, to compensate those crystal tits.
ISABELLE.
Monsieur, what of our marriage? Not to force you …
GERONTE.
My darling *Isabelle*, I here divorce you
And pass you in my stead to this bad seed —
Who'll blossom richly, thanks to this mad deed.
And given my sudden urge to dance and sing,
I don't care if the fairies wrote the thing.
So Scruple, file this instantly at court,
And pray excuse my having been so short.
(So to speak.) Blame that swoon. My head was spun.
SCRUPLE.
Oh, *may* I stay, please, for the denouement?
Why the suspense, monsieur, is killing me!
I know it seems absurd — unwilling me,
Lord Have-You-Seen-My-Ring-And-Golden-Chain,
Requesting more non-sequiturs, more pain.
But Christ, this place is fun! A wondrous mess!
I wish my every day knew such excess.
For I, who spend my days tilting for fees
Feel up on stilts instead of on my knees!
Oh, please, please, *please*. I'll be as still as clay.
GERONTE.
You're very strange.
SCRUPLE.
                    I am!

GERONTE.

All right, then, stay.

SCRUPLE.

Thank you!

GERONTE.

For wedded bliss is now our theme!

ERASTE.

But, sir, you only left us one centime.

GERONTE.

You ransacked my whole house, you heartless youth?

I'm only joking, lad, for here's the truth:

There's so much gold you'll run amok with it.

CRISPIN and ERASTE.

But *where?*

GERONTE.

That clock is chockablock with it!

ERASTE.

Your fortune's in its chronologic pocket?

GERONTE.

Drop in that old centime and you'll unlock it.

ALL.

Where is THE COIN?

ERASTE.

Out there!

(Eraste leaps out the window. Crispin imitates a sports announcer.)

CRISPIN.

More tension, folks,

As our young hero, caught in Fortune's spokes,

Looks for the damn centime!

(Eraste comes leaping back into the room, with the coin.)

ERASTE.

The coin is here!

CRISPIN.

I *told* you you should keep it!

ERASTE.

All stand clear!

(The clock whirs and begins its farting chime as Eraste takes the centime, drops it in a slot, and pulls a crank. Immediately, the strangled chime starts to ring out loud and clear — and a fortune in gold coins pours out, as if the clock were a one-armed bandit.)

97

ALL.

A million! A million! A million!

ERASTE.

So it was *here?*

GERONTE.

You didn't need to roam!

CRISPIN.

Well, like they say ...

CRISPIN, ERASTE, ISABELLE, and LISETTE. *(Clicking their heels, as in* The Wizard of Oz.*)*

There's no place like home, there's no place like home ...

MADAME ARGANTE.

But wait! This treasure straight from Tiffany
Has sparked in me a rare epiphany!
For see how money caused that strangled chime —
As down the ages *Gold* has strangled *Time!*
Clogged history's onward march with wars of greed,
Usurped the common good for private need,
Transforming me into a heartless vulture,
Who as a blushing maid craved art and culture.
Who played bad folk songs wearing purple tights,
Smoked weed, and argued for the people's rights!
Well, I'll no more be slave to money's chains,
But do what mere humanity ordains!
SOCIALISM!

(Tosses coins into the audience.)

GERONTE.

Eulalie ...

MADAME ARGANTE.

SOCIALISM NOW!

GERONTE.

This is America!

(Corrects himself.)

France! You'll start a row!

ISABELLE.

Amazing, Mom! Your character's been inverted!

MADAME ARGANTE.

Today I've been alchemically converted.

GERONTE.

So you abjure all use of legal tender?